普通高等教育"十二五"规划教材
全国高职高专项目课程系列教材

导游英语情景口语
（第二版）
Situational Spoken English for Tourist Guides

陈 欣 主编

内 容 简 介

《导游英语情景口语》（第二版）是针对高等职业技术学院培养涉外导游应用型人才而编写的教材。本着"以就业为导向，以能力为本位"的人才培养目标，其教学模式突出职业能力的训练与养成。本教材打破以知识传授为主体的传统学科课程模式，采用项目、模块编排方式，以导游工作任务为核心，同时突出"情景模拟"，注重听说能力的训练，让学生在模仿实践中通过完成具体项目来构建相关理论知识框架，并发展职业能力。

本书适合高职高专类院校旅游专业学生作为教材使用，也可供旅游从业人员参考阅读。

图书在版编目（CIP）数据

导游英语情景口语/陈欣主编．—2版．—北京：北京大学出版社，2012.7

（全国高职高专项目课程系列教材）

ISBN 978-7-301-20595-2

Ⅰ．导… Ⅱ．陈… Ⅲ．导游—英语—口语—高等职业教育—教材 Ⅳ．H319.9

中国版本图书馆 CIP 数据核字（2012）第 083433 号

书　　　　名：	导游英语情景口语（第二版）
著作责任者：	陈　欣　主编
策 划 编 辑：	胡伟晔
责 任 编 辑：	成　淼
标 准 书 号：	ISBN 978-7-301-20595-2/H・3049
出　版　者：	北京大学出版社
地　　　　址：	北京市海淀区成府路 205 号　100871
网　　　　址：	http://www.pup.cn
电　　　　话：	邮购部 010-62752015　发行部 010-62750672　编辑部 010-62704142
电 子 邮 箱：	编辑部 zyjy@pup.cn　总编室 zpup@pup.cn
印　刷　者：	北京虎彩文化传播有限公司
发　行　者：	北京大学出版社
经　销　者：	新华书店
	787 毫米×1092 毫米　16 开本　16.25 印张　395 千字
	2009 年 2 月第 1 版
	2012 年 7 月第 2 版　2024 年 1 月第 15 次印刷（总第 19 次印刷）
定　　　　价：	39.00 元（配 MP3 光盘 1 张）

未经许可，不得以任何方式复制或抄袭本书之部分或全部内容。

版权所有，侵权必究

举报电话：010-62752024；电子邮箱：fd@pup.cn

图书如有印装问题，请与出版部联系，电话：010-62756370

第二版前言

《导游英语情景口语》自出版以来，受到了广大师生和社会读者的普遍好评，被很多院校相关专业选为教材，也成为许多旅游从业者的必备工作手册，每年的销售量很大，且不断地在重印。

为了使本书内容更丰富，特色更鲜明，专业性更突出，我们对本书进行了全面的修订，努力使其更好地适应教学和社会的需要。本次修订仍沿用第一版的框架和主要内容，每个项目的口语练习增加了主题，以突出本书"口语"的特色。同时，为了丰富本书的内容，突出其专业特色，第二版特增加附录。附录部分是导游考试需要了解的基本知识，其内容包括中国各地名胜古迹、中国历史文化名城、国家重点风景名胜区、中国历史年代简表、中国十大菜系。

本书可供高职高专及以上水平的旅游专业教学使用，也可供旅游英语爱好者自学；同时，也可供旅游从业人员作为培训材料。

本书由宁波城市职业技术学院陈欣任主编，负责提出修订构思并具体编写、总纂、定稿和审稿，李文星和方义桂任副主编。

本次修订再次得到了同行业朋友们的热忱支持，参阅了大量相关资料，在此一并表示衷心的感谢！尽管我们在《导游英语情景口语》（第二版）修订工作方面做出了很多的努力，但由于能力和水平有限，不当之处还望读者指正。

宁波城市职业技术学院
陈　欣
2012 年 3 月

前　　言

中国是世界上最大的旅游市场之一，国内旅游市场已经达到15亿人次，出境旅游市场发展到4000多万人次，入境旅游市场达到一亿人次。全国旅行社接近两万家，全国旅游总收入已突破一万亿，入境旅游收入占旅游整体收入的25%左右。蓬勃发展的旅游业让我们意识到：旅游人才的培养尤其是优秀的涉外导游人才的培养是当前一项重要的任务。

《导游英语情景口语》是针对高等职业技术学院培养涉外导游应用型人才而编写的教材。高职类院校人才培养的定位是"以就业为导向，以能力为本位"，因此，其教学模式是突出职业能力的训练与养成。但是，针对涉外导游人才实践能力训练的教材在国内尚属罕见。为了填补这一空白，满足实际教学的需要，我们精心编写了这本教材，供大家选用。

本书力图打破以知识传授为主要特征的传统学科课程模式，将教学重心转变为以工作任务为核心的项目课程模式，让学生通过完成具体项目来构建相关理论知识框架，并发展职业能力。在结构设计上较传统教材有了一个创新性的改革，采用了项目、模块编排方式，强调了教材的职业性、实用性和趣味性。本书具有如下几个特点。

1．项目、模块与任务相结合：在每一个大项目下有若干个模块，每个模块下有要求学生完成的任务。

2．以导游实际工作程序为全书的编写体系：学生学好整本书后能够熟知导游工作流程且基本胜任涉外导游的工作。

3．突出听和说：每一个模块下都配有听说练习。

4．突出"情景模拟"：每一个模块下都有具体的情景实践模拟，并且给出具体操作步骤，方便学生学习掌握。

5．强调任务为核心：每一个模块都有具体的任务（Task），引导学生循序渐进地学习。

全书共16个项目，内容涵盖了从接机到送机的涉外导游服务工作全过程。其中，每一个项目下又由3+1个模块构成，前3个模块是根据涉外导游工作程序展开，第4个模块则是补充材料，有景点解说词、导游工作常识等。每个模块则包括以下几个任务（Task）。

Task 1: 热身练习（Warm-up）——形式多样，有相关主题讨论、词义猜想、景点翻译等。

Task 2: 常用词汇和句型学习（Learning Points）——所列的词汇和句型均是一线涉外导游工作中使用最为频繁的，非常具有典型性。与传统教材不同的是，本教材将相关对话或者文章的生词和句型作为重点提前呈现出来，旨在让学生在学习对话或者文章前就将其词汇和常用句型熟记于心。

Task 3: 旅游情景会话（Dialogue）——内容涉及涉外导游服务的工作程序，具有较强的实用性和可操作性。

Task 4: 听力练习（Listen and Answer）——根据上面的对话内容提5个问题，同时要求学生通过听录音将问题写出来并回答，这样既锻炼了听说，也锻炼了口语。

Task 5: 角色演练（Role-play）——根据相关主题设置导游实际工作场景，要求学生根据情景操练。其中，Situation A 有具体的条目，方便学生练习；Situation B 和 C 则是拓展练习。

本书配有所有对话、文章和听力的录音光盘，由美籍专业人士录制，语音纯正，情景性强，便于模仿。教师用书为电子版，如有需要，可与出版社联系。联系方式为 zyjy@pup.cn。

本书可供高职高专及以上水平的旅游专业教学使用，也可供旅游英语爱好者自学；同时，还可供旅游从业人员作为培训材料。

本书参编人员及编写单元如下：陈欣（项目1、5、6、10）；李文星（项目2、3、4）；方义桂（项目7、8、9）；许文婧（项目11、15、16）；滕汉华（项目12、13、14）。其中，陈欣任本书主编，并拟定编写大纲和统稿，方义桂和李文星任副主编。

本书在编写过程中，得到了同行业朋友们的热忱支持，还参阅了大量相关资料，在此一并表示衷心的感谢！尽管我们在《导游英语情景口语》的特色建设方面做出了很多的努力，但由于能力和水平有限，不当之处还望读者指正。

宁波城市职业技术学院
陈　欣
2008 年 12 月

Contents 目录

Item 1 Meeting Guests 迎接客人 1
- Model 1 Meeting Guests at the Airport 接机服务 2
- Model 2 On the Way to the Hotel 至饭店途中 5
- Model 3 A Welcome Speech 欢迎词 9
- Model 4 China—a Country with an Ancient Civilization 古国话文明 11

Item 2 Hotel Check-in 饭店入住登记 15
- Model 1 Hotel Room Reservation 预定客房 16
- Model 2 Checking in 入住登记 19
- Model 3 Itinerary Planning 行程安排 22
- Model 4 Process of Hotel Guest Registration 基本入住登记程序 25

Item 3 Housekeeping Service 客房服务 30
- Model 1 Escorting the Guest into the Guest Room 陪送客人进房 31
- Model 2 Making Up the Room 收拾房间 34
- Model 3 About Room Service Order 客房用餐服务 37
- Model 4 Hotels Today 今日酒店 40

Item 4 Food & Beverage Service 餐饮服务 44
- Model 1 Reserving a Table 预定餐桌 45
- Model 2 Helping to Order Dishes 帮助点菜 48
- Model 3 The Payment 付款 51
- Model 4 The Chinese Food 中国饮食 54

Item 5 City Sightseeing and Transportation 都市观光和交通 59
- Model 1 City Tours 都市游 60
- Model 2 Car Rental Service 租车服务 63
- Model 3 Xikou of Fenghua 奉化溪口 67

Item 6 The Service of Travel Destinations 旅游目的地服务 72
- Model 1 Narrations on Tour 沿途讲解 73
- Model 2 At the Ticket Box 在售票处 76
- Model 3 Asking the Way 问路 79
- Model 4 The Role of a Tour Guide 导游的职责 82

Item 7 Tour of Gardens 园林游览 86
- Model 1 A Trip to the Yu Yuan Garden 游览豫园 87
- Model 2 Touring the Summer Palace 游览颐和园 91
- Model 3 The Four Elements in a Traditional Garden 园林四要素 95
- Model 4 Suzhou Gardens 苏州园林 99

Item 8	Tour of Mountains 山、水之旅	104
Model 1	On Huangshan 黄山之旅	105
Model 2	A Trip in Guilin 游览桂林	109
Model 3	Huangguoshu Waterfalls 黄果树瀑布	113
Model 4	West Lake 西湖	116

Item 9	Tour of Temples 中国庙宇	121
Model 1	Visiting the Jade Buddha Temple 游览玉佛寺	122
Model 2	Daoism 道教	126
Model 3	Visiting the Confucius Temple 孔子庙	131
Model 4	Visiting the Wudang Mountain 游览武当山	135

Item 10	Tours of Historical Sites 名胜古迹之旅	141
Model 1	A Tour of the Forbidden City 游览紫禁城	142
Model 2	The Tour of the Great Wall 长城之旅	145
Model 3	The Tianyi Pavilion Library 天一阁藏书楼	149

Item 11	Tour of Chinese Characteristic Culture 中国特色文化之旅	153
Model 1	Taijiquan 太极拳	154
Model 2	Spring Festival 春节	157
Model 3	Beijing Opera 京剧	160
Model 4	China—Home of Tea 茶乡中国	164

Item 12	Shopping 旅游购物	169
Model 1	Chinese Calligraphy 中国书法	170
Model 2	Antiques and Ancient Furniture 古玩家具	173
Model 3	At the Souvenir Shop 在纪念品商店	176
Model 4	Jade Culture 玉器文化	179

Item 13	Handling Problems & Emergencies 处理问题与紧急情况	184
Model 1	A Lost Passport 遗失护照	185
Model 2	Calling the First Aid Center 打电话到急救中心	187
Model 3	First Aid Techniques 急救技术	190

Item 14	Handling Customer Complaints 顾客投诉处理服务	194
Model 1	A Delayed Flight 航班延误	195
Model 2	Complaining about the food 食品投诉	198
Model 3	A Tour Guide or a Shopping Guide 导游还是导购	200
Model 4	A Complaint Letter on Holiday Booking 旅游度假投诉信	203

Item 15	Checking Out 结账退房服务	207
Model 1	Paying the Hotel Bill in Cash 现金付账	208
Model 2	Paying with Credit Card 信用卡付账	211
Model 3	Paying with a Traveler's Check 支票付账	214
Model 4	Checkout Service Procedures 退房结账程序	217

Item 16　Farewell, China　再见，中国 ·· 221
　　　Model 1　See You Again Soon　再见 ·· 222
　　　Model 2　Seeing Guests off at the Airport　机场送客 ·········· 225
　　　Model 3　A Farewell Speech　欢送词 ·· 228
Appendix 1　Scenic Spots and Historical Sites in China　中国各地名胜古迹 ········ 233
Appendix 2　Famous Chinese Historical and Cultural Cities　中国历史文化名城 ····· 239
Appendix 3　The National Key Attractions and Scenic Spots　国家重点风景名胜区 ······· 241
Appendix 4　A Brief Chinese Chronology　中国历史年代简表 ················· 245
Appendix 5　The Ten Different Cooking Styles in China　中国十大菜系 ······· 247
References　参考书目 ·· 249

Item 1 Meeting Guests

迎 接 客 人

Model 1:
   Meeting Guests at the Airport 接机服务

Model 2:
   On the Way to the Hotel 至饭店途中

Model 3:
   A Welcome Speech 欢迎词

Model 4:
   China-a Country with an Ancient Civilization
   古国话文明

Model 1
Meeting Guests at the Airport 接机服务

Task 1

Warm-up

Work in pairs. Learn the following words of the travel industry. Then answer the questions below.

airlines	travel agency	front office	housekeeping department
food and beverage department		scenic spots	shopping arcade

1. Think of two jobs in each sector.
2. Which of these jobs interest you the most? Why?

Task 2

Learning Points

Listen to the following *words* and *useful expressions* and repeat. Then try to memorize them.

Words and Phrases

lobby	['lɔbi]	n.	（机场）大厅
guide	[gaid]	n.	导游
Los Angeles	[lɔs'ændʒələs]	n.	[美]洛杉矶市
tired	['taiəd]	adj.	累的，疲劳的
nevertheless	[ˌnevəðə'les]	conj.	然而，不过
interesting	['intristiŋ]	adj.	有趣的
luggage	['lʌgidʒ]	n.	行李
travel service			旅行社
tourist group			旅游团
I can manage			我能应付
shuttle bus			短程往返运送的公共汽车
parking lot			停车场

Meeting Guests   Item 1

Useful Expressions

1. Welcome to China!
   欢迎您到中国来!
2. Did you have a good trip?
   旅行愉快吗?
3. You all need a good rest first.
   你们都需要先休息一下。
4. You will have plenty of time to see all the interesting places in China.
   你们会有很多时间欣赏中国的著名景点。
5. Is everyone in the group here?
   全团的人都在吗?
6. Shall I help you with your luggage?
   让我来帮您拿行李好吗?
7. The shuttle bus is just waiting in the parking lot.
   大巴正在停车场等位。

Task 3

Dialogue I

Listen to the *dialogue I* for the first time. Then practise the dialogue by reading it aloud with your partner. Read through it at least twice, changing your role each time.

Meeting Guests at the Airport

【Scene】 *In the airport lobby, Meng Jun, a young tour guide from the Youth Travel Service, is greeting a tourist group from the United States headed by James Green.*

M: Meng Jun   J: James Green

M: Excuse me! Are you Mr. Green from Los Angeles?
J: Yes, I'm James Green.
M: Nice to meet you, Mr. Green. I'm Meng Jun, your tour guide from the Youth Travel Service. Just call me Jun.
J: Nice to meet you, too.
M: (Meng Jun shakes hands with Mr. Green and other guests) **Welcome to China!**
J: We're so glad you've come to meet us at the airport, Jun.
M: **Did you have a good trip**, Mr. Green?
J: Yes, quite pleasant. But we feel a bit tired after the long flight.

M: Yes, you must. **You all need a good rest first**.

J: Nevertheless we are all excited that we've finally arrived in the country that we have been wishing to see for years.

M: **You will have plenty of time to see all the interesting places in China. Is everyone in the group here?**

J: Yes, a party of ten. We have five ladies and five gentlemen.

M: Good. Can we go now? **Shall I help you with your luggage**, Mr. Green?

J: No, thanks. I can manage.

M: Please follow me, ladies and gentlemen! **The shuttle bus is just waiting in the parking lot.**

J: That's fine. Hurry up, guys!

M: This way, please.

Task 4

Listen and Answer

You will hear five questions. Listen carefully and give an appropriate answer to each of them.

(1) _____
(2) _____
(3) _____
(4) _____
(5) _____

Task 5

Role-play

Act out the following dialogs.

【Situation A】 The local guide from China Youth Travel Service is at the airport to meet an inbound travel group from USA. Mr. Jones is the tour leader.

Local guide:
- ☆ Greets Mr. Jones and extends welcome to him.
- ☆ Asks about the flight.
- ☆ Thinks that Mr. Jones is possibly tired.
- ☆ Asks Mr. Jones if all members of his party are all here.
- ☆ Offers to help with the baggage.

Meeting Guests   Item 1

- ☆ Says a bus will send them to the hotel.

Mr. Jones:
- ☆ Greets the local guide.
- ☆ Says the flight was a bit long.
- ☆ Answers that he had some sleep during the flight.
- ☆ Tells his wish for this trip.
- ☆ Tells the number of people in the group.
- ☆ Expresses thanks. Says he can take care of his baggage himself.

【Situation B】 You are a local guide from China International Travel Service. You are at the airport to meet tour group of 50 people. The tour escort is Mr. Hu.

【Situation C】 At the railway station, the tour guide from local travel agency meets a foreign traveler.

Model 2
On the Way to the Hotel 至饭店途中

Task 1

Warm-up

Work in pairs. Learn the following words of the industry. Then answer the questions below.

| safari park | festival | amusement park |
| historic building | place of natural beauty | |

Which of these tourist attractions would interest you the most? Why?

Task 2

Learning Points

Listen to the following *words* and *useful expressions* and repeat. Then try to memorize them.

Words and Phrases

tourist   ['tuərist]   n.   游客

international	[ˌɪntə(ː)ˈnæʃənəl]	adj.	国际的
enjoyable	[ɪnˈdʒɔɪəb(ə)l]	adj.	令人愉快的，有乐趣的
memorable	[ˈmemərəbl]	adj.	值得纪念的，难忘的
swan	[swɔn]	n.	天鹅
efficient	[ɪˈfɪʃənt]	adj.	有效率的
extensive	[ɪksˈtensɪv]	adj.	广大的，广泛的，全面的
facility	[fəˈsɪlɪtɪ]	n.	(pl -ies) 设施，设备
dine	[daɪn]	v.	吃饭，进餐
entertain	[ˌentəˈteɪn]	v.	款待，使娱乐
square	[skwɛə]	n.	广场
monument	[ˈmɔnjumənt]	n.	纪念碑
magnificent	[mægˈnɪfɪsnt]	adj.	宏伟的
reception	[rɪˈsepʃən]	n.	(旅馆)接待处
scenic spots			景点
historical sites			名胜古迹
The Great Wall			长城
The Palace Museum			故宫
The Summer Palace			颐和园
reception desk			接待柜台

Useful Expressions

1. Is everybody on the bus?
   每个人都在车上了吗？

2. Shall we go now?
   我们现在可以出发了吗？

3. Let me introduce my team to you first.
   首先让我来向大家介绍一下我的团队。

4. We will do our best to make your trip more enjoyable and memorable.
   我们将尽最大努力使你们的旅行更有趣、更难忘。

5. It's one of the best four-star hotels in the city.
   它是这个城市最好的四星级酒店之一。

6. I hope you will enjoy your stay there.
   我希望你能在那住得愉快。

7. Next, I'd like to introduce something about this city.
   接下来，我想要介绍一下有关这个城市的一些情况。

8. There're many famous scenic spots and historical sites in Beijing.
   在北京有很多著名的景点和名胜古迹。

9. I'm afraid you need a good rest first.
   恐怕你得先休息。

10. Let's get off and go to the reception desk.
    让我们下车去接待处。

Task 3

Dialogue II

Listen to the *dialogue II* for the first time. Then practise the dialogue by reading it aloud with your partner. Read through it at least twice, changing your role each time.

On the Way to the Hotel

【Scene】 *Zhu Wei, the guide, met the tour group at the airport and they are driving to the hotel. The coach is about to start.*

> Z: Zhu Wei   T: tourist

Z: **Is everybody on the bus**?
T: Yes, I think so.
Z: **Shall we go now**?
T: Yes, please.
Z: (to all the tourists in the coach) Welcome to China, ladies and gentlemen. **Let me introduce my team to you first**. My name is Zhu Wei. I am a tour guide from China International Travel Service. I'll be with you for your trip in Beijing. This is Mr. Fang, our driver. **We will do our best to make your trip more enjoyable and memorable.** I hope you will have a very pleasant stay here in Beijing. Thank you very much! Now, we are driving straight to the hotel, the White Swan Hotel.
T: Well, how far is it to the hotel?
Z: It'll take us about one hour. **It's one of the best four-star hotels in the city.** There is warm and efficient service with extensive leisure facilities. **I hope you will enjoy your stay there.**
T: That's great.
Z: **Next, I'd like to introduce something about this city**. Beijing is the capital of China. It is a pleasant place to visit as well as to do business, shop, dine, or be entertained. **There're many famous scenic spots and historical sites in Beijing,** such as the Great Wall, the Palace Museum, the Summer Palace, and so on.
T: We are really longing for a visit.
Z: You must be tired after the long trip. **I'm afraid you need a good rest first.**
T: That's very kind of you. Oh, look, what a big square!

Z: Yes, it is Tian'anmen. It is perhaps one of the largest squares in the world today.
T: That's rather interesting. What about that building?
Z: It is the Monument to the People's Heroes.
T: I see, it looks magnificent.
Z: Well, here we are. This is the hotel. **Let's get off and go to the reception desk.**
T: OK.

Task 4

Listen and Answer

You will hear five questions. Listen carefully and give an appropriate answer to each of them.

(1) _____
(2) _____
(3) _____
(4) _____
(5) _____

Task 5

Role-play

Act out the following dialogs.

【Situation A】 You are an English tour guide who is meeting an American tour group at the airport in Hangzhou. On the way to the hotel, you are supposed:
  ☆ to make a welcome speech.
  ☆ to say something about the hotel.
  ☆ to brief on the city.
  ☆ to explain the scene along the way.
Discuss with your partner, and then speak it by yourself.

【Situation B】 You, a local guide, met a tour group at the bus station in Ningbo. On the way to the hotel, you are introducing Ningbo to your tourists.

Meeting Guests　　Item 1

Model 3
A Welcome Speech　欢迎词

Task 1

Warm-up

Work in pairs. If you are a guide, when you meet your guests for the first time, what will you say to them? Discuss with your partner.

Task 2

Learning Points

Listen to the following *words* and *useful expressions* and repeat. Then try to memorize them.

Words and Phrases

speech	[spi:tʃ]	n.	发言，演说
surname	[ˈsə:neim]	n.	姓氏
experience	[iksˈpiəriəns]	n.	经验，经历
suggestion	[səˈdʒestʃən]	n.	建议
hesitate	[ˈheziteit]	v.	犹豫
swan	[swɔn]	n.	天鹅
lobby	[ˈlɔbi]	n.	大堂
remember	[riˈmembə]	v.	记住

Useful Expressions

1. Allow me to introduce myself.
   请允许我在这里作一下自我介绍。
2. And this is Mr. Deng, our driver, who has had 10 years of driving experience.
   这是我们的司机邓师傅，他有着10年的驾龄。
3. We'll do everything possible to make your visit a pleasant experience.
   我们将竭诚使你们一路游览愉快。
4. If you have any problems or suggestions, please don't hesitate to let us know.
   如果你们有任何问题或者建议话，请尽管告诉我们。

5. Please do remember the plate number of our bus.
请务必记住我们的车牌号。

Task 3

Passage Reading I

Listen to the short passage for the first time. Then practise it by reading it aloud by yourself.

A Welcome Speech

Good morning, ladies and gentlemen, Welcome to China. **Allow me to introduce myself.** My name is Huang Lan. Huang is my surname, so you may call me Xiao Huang. I'm a guide from Zhejiang China Travel Service. **And this is Mr. Deng, our driver, who has had 10 years of driving experience.** We're glad to have all of you here.

I'll be with you during your five-day tour in this city and we'll be at your service at any time. **We'll do everything possible to make your visit a pleasant experience. If you have any problems or suggestions, please don't hesitate to let us know.**

The hotel where you stay is the White Swan Hotel. It offers the best services in this city. We shall meet at the hotel lobby at 7:00 a.m. for our first visit tomorrow. **Please do remember the plate number of our bus.** The number is 192588. Thank you.

We hope you'll enjoy your stay in this city.

Task 4

Listen and Answer

You will hear five questions. Listen carefully and give an appropriate answer to each of them.

(1) _____
(2) _____
(3) _____
(4) _____
(5) _____

Task 5

Speaking

Make a "Welcome Speech" with your partner.

Meeting Guests Item 1

Model 4
China—a Country with an Ancient Civilization 古国话文明

Task 1

Learning Points

Listen to the following *words* and *useful expressions* and repeat. Then try to memorize them.

Words and Phrases

ancient	[ˈeinʃənt]	adj.	古老的，古代的
civilization	[ˌsivilaiˈzeiʃən;-liˈz-]	n.	文明
inventor	[inˈventə(r)]	n.	发明者
compass	[ˈkʌmpəs]	n.	指南针
printing	[ˈprintiŋ]	n.	印刷术
resource	[riˈsɔːs]	n.	（常作 pl）资源
elegant	[ˈeligənt]	adj.	雅致的，优美的
waterfalls	[ˈwɔːtəfɔːlz]	n.	瀑布
rare	[rɛə]	adj.	稀有的，罕见的
species	[ˈspiːʃiz]	n.	（常作 pl）（生物）种，种类
distinctive	[disˈtiŋktiv]	adj.	有特色的，特别的
cuisine	[kwi(ː)ˈziːn]	n.	烹饪
domestic	[dəˈmestik]	adj.	家的，本国的
political	[pəˈlitikəl]	adj.	国家的，政治的
contemporary	[kənˈtempərəri]	adj.	当代的，现代的
cultural relics			文化遗迹
historical sites			名胜古迹
look forward to (doing)			期待（做）

Useful Expressions

1. China has a written history of over 5,000 years of civilization and boasts rich cultural relics and historical sites.
   中国有着五千多年的灿烂文化和丰富的历史文化遗迹。
2. China attracts a large number of domestic and foreign tourists every year.

中国每年都吸引着大量的国内外游客。
3. Beijing, the capital city of the People's Republic of China, is the country's political and cultural center.
中华人民共和国的首都——北京，是国家的政治和文化中心。
4. Beijing, as well as the whole country of China, is looking forward to welcoming friends from all over the world!
北京，以及全中国都在翘首盼望着迎接来自世界各地的朋友们！

Task 2

Passage Reading II

Listen to the short passage for the first time. Then practise it by reading it aloud by yourself.

China—a Country with an Ancient Civilization

China has a written history of over 5,000 years of civilization and boasts rich cultural relics and historical sites. It is the inventor of compass, papermaking, gunpowder and printing. Thanks to China's rich tourist resources ——high mountains, elegant river, springs and waterfalls, rich and varied folk customs, rare species, scenic spots and historical sites, distinctive opera, music and dance, and world-famous cuisine, **China attracts a large number of domestic and foreign tourists every year.**

Beijing, the capital city of the People's Republic of China, is the country's political and cultural center. It is also one of the world's most famous historical and cultural cities where you can learn the 1,000 year contemporary history of the country.

Beijing, as well as the whole country of China, is looking forward to welcoming friends from all over the world!

Task 3

Listen and Answer

You will hear five questions. Listen carefully and give an appropriate answer to each of them.
(1) _____
(2) _____
(3) _____
(4) _____
(5) _____

Meeting Guests   Item 1

Task 4

Oral Practice

Retell the text in your own words.

Task 5

More Oral and Listening Practice:
【Listening】 Listen to the following dialog & passage and fill in the blanks.

Listening I

At the Airport

A: _____?
B: Why, yes, I'm Mark Davis.
A: Oh, Mr. Davis._____.
_____.
B: Hello, Ms Zhu. Thank you for coming to meet us.
A: Welcome to China Mr. Davis. _____ ?
B: Fine. We had a very pleasant flight, _____,
my assistant. She is in charge of the daily affairs of our tour party.
A: How do you do, Miss Tyler? _____.
B: How do you do? I'm pleased to meet you, too.
A: We've made reservations for your party at the Hong Kong Garden Hotel.
B: Thank you very much.
A: Shall_____?_____outside.
B: Fine.
A: Your_____in the hotel.
B: That's good.
A: _____, Mr. Davis?
B: It's very kind of you.

Listening II

Traveling in Beijing

There are many fascinating sights in and_____Beijing, but

before visiting the attractions, _____ an hour or two walking the streets. _____ off the main boulevards and _____ through the mazelike alleys where _____ residents live or perhaps stroll down Old Culture Street. If your hotel is _____, walk to the walled 14th-century Forbidden City, so _____ because it was off limits to ordinary citizens. On its grounds are six _____ and 800 smaller buildings, containing _____ rooms. The main gate of the palace opens onto Tiananmen Square. The square is the _____ of the _____ to the People's Heroes, Mao Zedong's Mausoleum, the _____ of the People, the Museum of Chinese _____; the Museum of the Chinese _____.

【Topics】 Divide the class into groups. Choose one of the following topics to discuss in each group. Give a short report about the group's opinion after that.

1. What do you think the definition of tourism is?
2. Do you think our daily lives will be greatly affected by the development of tourism? Why or why not?
3. Which is your favorite way of traveling, package tour or independent traveling? Why?

Item 2 Hotel Check-in

饭店入住登记

Model 1:
  Hotel Room Reservation　预定客房

Model 2:
  Checking in　入住登记

Model 3:
  Itinerary Planning　行程安排

Model 4:
  Process of Hotel Guest Registration
  基本入住登记程序

Model 1
Hotel Room Reservation 预定客房

Task 1

Warm-up

Work in pairs. Learn the following words of the sectors of the hotel services. Then answer the questions below.

reserve	hotel	inn	star-hotel
single	double deluxe	bath	shower

1. When you are arranging for a room reservation, what information should you include?
2. Name different types of hotels. What is the main difference among these different types of hotels?
3. Discuss the different types of rooms of a hotel.

Task 2

Learning Points

Listen to the following *words* and *useful expressions* and repeat. Then try to memorize them.

Words and Phrases

client	['klaiənt]	n.	顾客，客户，委托人
luxurious	[lʌg'zjuəriəs]	adj.	奢侈的，豪华的
reservation	[,rezə'veiʃən]	n.	（旅馆房间）预定
deluxe	[di'lʌks, di'luks]	adj.	豪华的，华丽的
presidential	[,prezi'denʃəl]	adj.	总统的
confirm	[kən'fə:m]	v.	确认
suite	[swi:t]	n.	（一套）家具，套房

Useful Expressions

1. This is Hu Hong, the tour guide of China Youth Travel Agency.

Hotel Check-in   Item 2

我是中国青年旅行社的导游胡红。

2. I'd like to reserve a room in Guangzhou.
   我想在广州预定一个房间。
3. What kind of room would you like to reserve?
   请问您想要预订什么样的房间？
4. How long would you stay here?
   请问您要住几天？
5. There would be some discount when the hotel is not very busy.
   如果酒店不是很忙，可以打折。
6. Is there anything else I can do for you?
   请问还有别的事吗？
7. Just call me when you have other questions.
   如果有其他问题，请呼叫我。

Task 3

Dialogue I

Listen to the *dialogue I* for the first time. Then practice the dialogue by reading it aloud with your partner. Read through it at least twice, changing your role each time.

Hotel Room Reservation

G: guide   C: client

G: **This is Hu Hong, the tour guide of China Youth Travel Agency.** Can I help you?

C: This is John Smith from London. **I'd like to reserve a room in Guangzhou.** Will you please arrange it for me?

G: It's my pleasure. **What kind of room would you like to reserve?** We have singles, doubles, suites of different styles, deluxe ones.

C: A British suite, please.

G: OK. **How long would you stay here**?

C: Three days from the third to the fifth of March.

G: Now, Mr. Smith, let's check the information. You'd like to reserve a British suite for three days from the third to the fifth of March. Is that so?

C: Yes, exactly.

G: **Is there anything else I can do for you**?

C: Can you give some idea about the price for the hotel?

17

G: Well, it's about 1000 RMB for one day. And **there would be some discount when the hotel is not very busy**.
C: OK. I see. Thank you for the information.
G: Thank you for calling. We look forward to seeing you. **Just call me when you have other questions.**
C: Thank you. Bye!
G: Good bye.

Task 4

Listen and Answer

You will hear five questions. Listen carefully and give an appropriate answer to each of them.

(1) _____
(2) _____
(3) _____
(4) _____
(5) _____

Task 5

Role-play

Act out the following dialogs.

【Situation A】 Wu Fei, a tour guide of Rainbow Travel Agency is receiving the phone. Eleanor Swan is a foreign guest who wants to make a reservation through Rainbow Travel Agency. They are having a conversation about the reservation.

Guide:
☆ Upon receiving the call, greets Eleanor Swan and makes a self-introduction.
☆ Offers help.
☆ Tells the different kinds of rooms and their respective prices.
☆ Asks the kind of room Eleanor Swan would like to reserve.
☆ Asks the date Eleanor Swan would like to stay.
☆ Asks to check the information.
☆ Says good-bye and express good wishes.

Client:
☆ Greets the guide and gives a self-introduction.
☆ Asks to reserve a room.

Hotel Check-in   Item 2

☆ Asks the different prices of different rooms.
☆ Asks to reserve a double-room with a bath.
☆ Tells the date he/she would stay.
☆ Confirms the information with guide.
☆ Expresses thanks.

【Situation B】A Chinese tour guide makes a group reservation for 28 guests to stay in New York for two days.

【Situation C】A French travel agency asks a Chinese tour guide to reserve a room for Mr. Steve to stay in Nanjing for three days.

Model 2
Checking in   入住登记

Task 1

Warm-up

Work in pairs. Learn the following words of the travel industry. Then answer the question below.

| museum | theatre | gallery | church or temple |
| residence of a famous person | | downtown | recreational center |

What place would you recommend to the tourists when you escort them to a new city? Why?

Task 2

Learning Points

Listen to the following *words* and *useful expressions* and repeat. Then try to memorize them.

Words and Phrases

Sino-Germany	[ˈsainəu dʒəːmən]	n.	中德
Delegation	[ˌdeliˈgeiʃən]	n.	代表团
name-list	[ˈneimlist]	n.	名单
well-prepared	[ˈwel priˈpɛəd]	adj.	准备充分的

voucher	['vaʊtʃə]	n.	凭证，[美]优惠购货卷
twin rooms			双人对床房
group visa			团体签证
morning-call service			叫醒服务
breakfast buffet			自助早餐

Useful Expressions

1. May I help you?
   有什么可以帮你吗？
2. We'd like to check in.
   我们要办理登记入住。
3. Do you have reservations?
   你们有预定吗？
4. A moment, please.
   请稍等。
5. Here is the name-list with the group visa.
   这是我们的名单和集体签证。
6. Here are the vouchers for your breakfast buffet.
   这是你们的早餐券。
7. Wish you a nice stay here.
   祝你们住（玩）得开心。

Task 3

Dialogue II

Listen to the *dialogue II* for the first time. Then practise the dialogue by reading it aloud with your partner. Read through it at least twice, changing your role each time.

Checking in

【Scene】 *The tour guide is helping a group of foreign visitors to check in at a hotel in Shanghai. The reception clerk receives the tour guide.*

C: clerk   G: guide

C: Good morning, madam. **May I help you?**
G: Yes, please. **We'd like to check in.**
C: **Do you have reservations**?
G: Yes. The Shanghai Youth Travel Agency has booked 15 rooms for us.
C: Would you please tell me the name of your group?

Hotel Check-in   Item 2

G: The Sino-German Friendship Bridge Delegation.
C: **A moment, please.**
   (*The clerk looks up the computer*)
C: Yes, 15 twin rooms for four nights.
G: Yes, exactly. **Here is the name-list with the group visa.**
C: Thank you. You are well-prepared. Here are the keys to the rooms. Do you need morning call service?
G: Yes, please make it at 7:00 a.m. for tomorrow morning and 8:00 a.m. for the rest of the days.
C: **Here are the vouchers for your breakfast buffet.** The breakfast will be served at the dining hall on the second floor from 7:00 to 9:00 a.m..
G: Thank you.
C: Thank you and **wish you a nice stay here**.

Task 4

Listen and Answer

You will hear five questions. Listen carefully and give an appropriate answer to each of them.

(1) _____
(2) _____
(3) _____
(4) _____
(5) _____

Task 5

Role-play

Act out the following dialogs.

【Situation A】 An English tour guide is leading a Chinese tour group to a five-star hotel in a foreign city. He is helping the group to check in. There is a conversation between the guide and the clerk of the hotel.

Clerk:
- ☆ Greets the guide and offers help.
- ☆ Asks whether the guide has a reservation.
- ☆ Asks the guide to wait a moment while checking the reservation on the computer, (Upon finding the reservation) confirms the reservation.

- ☆ Says the group should show their passports and visas.
- ☆ (Gives the keys to the rooms) Tells the floor and rooms.
- ☆ Reminds the group of security and the deposit money or other valuable things for free.
- ☆ Wishes the group to have a happy stay.

Tour guide:

- ☆ Greets the clerk and makes a self-introduction.
- ☆ Says the group has a reservation.
- ☆ Confirms the reservation that they would stay in the hotel for 4 days.
- ☆ Collects the groups' passports and visas and gives them to the clerk.
- ☆ Tells the group to choose rooms by themselves then make a list and gives it to the clerk.
- ☆ Thanks and tells the information to the group.
- ☆ Expresses thanks and says good-bye.

【Situation B】 A tour escort of a group from Canada is to help the group to check in. You are the local tour guide to receive the group. Make a conversation concerning the process of check-in. A third person can be invited to act as the clerk of the hotel.

Model 3
Itinerary Planning 行程安排

Task 1

Warm-up

Work in pairs. If you are a guide in Beijing, when you tell your guests the itinerary of a three-day city tour, what will you say to them? Discuss it with your partner.

Task 2

Learning Points

Listen to the following *words* and *useful expressions* and repeat. Then try to memorize them.

Words and Phrases

itinerary	[aiˈtinərəri]	n.	路线
accompany	[əˈkʌmpəni]	v.	陪同

Hotel Check-in   Item 2

pedestrian	[pəˈdestriən]	adj.	步行的
conducted	[kɔnˈdʌkt,-dəkt]	adj.	陪同的
memorial	[miˈmɔːriəl]	n.	纪念碑
sightseeing	[ˈsaitsiːiŋ]	n.	观光
vehicle	[ˈviːikl]	n.	交通工具，车辆
crystal	[ˈkristl]	n.	水晶

Useful Expressions

1. Hello everybody, can everyone hear me?
   大家都能听到我的话吗？
2. I'd like to say something about tomorrow's arrangement.
   我想说一下明天的行程安排。
3. The tour starts at 9 o'clock tomorrow morning and lasts about two hours.
   明天上午九点出游，大约游玩两个小时。
4. We'll meet outside the hotel entrance at about ten to nine.
   我们八点五十酒店门口集合。
5. There are some sightseeing vehicles available here and there.
   随处都有观光车可以坐。
6. The tour will end at the Crystal Teahouse in the main square.
   旅游终点在位于主广场的水晶茶馆。
7. I hope you will enjoy the tour.
   希望大家玩得开心。

Task 3

Dialogue III

Listen to the *dialogue III* for the first time. Then practise the dialogue by reading it aloud with your partner. Read through it at least twice, changing your role each time.

Itinerary Planning

A: tour guide   B: tour group or one of them

A: **Hello everybody, can everyone hear me?**
B: Yes, very clearly!
A: Thank you. **I'd like to say something about tomorrow's arrangement.**
B: Yeah! Go ahead.
A: I'll accompany you on a conducted tour round the city tomorrow.
B: Yes.

A: **The tour starts at 9 o'clock tomorrow morning and lasts about two hours.**
B: What time should we be ready?
A: Please be ready at 8: 50. **We'll meet outside the hotel entrance at about ten to nine.** Is that OK?
B: OK, ten to nine.
A: I suggest you bring your sunglasses, umbrella, and a hat as the weather is sunny.
B: Yes, thank you. How should we go?
A: We'll pay a visit to the Grand Theatre first. We'll go there by coach.
B: What will we do next?
A: We'll walk through the pedestrian mall on Nanjing Road and then visit the fruit and vegetable market.
B: Wonderful! I just want to buy some fresh fruit.
A: Then we'll pass by the heroes' memorial and walk along the river.
B: So, we need to walk a lot.
A: Well, it depends. **There are some sightseeing vehicles available here and there.**
B: That's great!
A: **The tour will end at the Crystal Teahouse in the main square.** There you'll be able to enjoy our famous local cake.
B: Wonderful!
A: **I hope you will enjoy the tour.** See you in the morning.

Task 4

Listen and Answer

You will hear five questions. Listen carefully and give an appropriate answer to each of them.
(1) _____
(2) _____
(3) _____
(4) _____
(5) _____

Task 5

Role-play

Act out the following dialogs.

Hotel Check-in   Item 2

【Situation A】 Make an itinerary plan around the city Hangzhou to include Lingyin Temple and the West Lake with your partner.

Tour guide:
☆ Greets the guests.
☆ Says the next day they'll visit Lingyin Temple and the West Lake.
☆ Tells the time and place to meet.
☆ Tells the time to the two places respectively and how long the tour lasts.
☆ Tells the things to prepare according to the weather.
☆ Says the lunch will be taken in a snack bar.
☆ Says they would go by coach.
☆ Tells the time to return the hotel.
☆ Thanks for attention and wishes them a nice tour.

Guest(s):
☆ Greets the guide.
☆ Agrees warmly for longing for the famous places.
☆ Asks the time and place to meet.
☆ Asks how long the tour will last.
☆ Asks what to prepare.
☆ Asks where to have lunch.
☆ Asks how they would go to the two places.
☆ Asks when they would go back to the hotel.
☆ Thanks for the information.

【Situation B】 Make a conversation about an itinerary plan with your partner. You can choose different cities or areas, but you should include at least two scenic spots.

Model 4
Process of Hotel Guest Registration 基本入住登记程序

Task 1

Learning Points

Listen to the following *words* and *useful expressions* and repeat. Then try to memorize them.

Words and Phrases

approach   [ə'prətʃ]   v.   走近

establish	[isˈtæbliʃ]	v.	确立，建立
title	[ˈtaitl]	n.	称呼
assign	[əˈsain]	v.	分配
deposit	[diˈpɔzit]	n.	押金
cardholder	[ˈkɑːd،həuldə(r)]	n.	持卡人
validity	[vəˈliditi]	n.	有效
receipt	[riˈsiːt]	n.	收据
cashier	[kəˈʃiə]	n.	收银员
eye contact			目光接触

Useful Expressions

1. Greet each guest with a smile in your voice as well as on your face.
   向客人问好时不仅要面带微笑，声音里也应该透着微笑。
2. You should first establish and keep eye contact with the guest.
   要首先和客人有目光接触。
3. When addressing the guest, do not call a guest by his or her first name.
   称呼客人，不可直呼其名。
4. Ask the guest to show his or her credit card for an imprint or to pay a deposit.
   让客人出示信用卡以复印，或者让他交押金。

Task 2

Passage Reading

Listen to the short passage for the first time. Then practise it by reading it aloud by yourself.

Process of Hotel Guest Registration

If you are a reception clerk at the reception desk, you should always **greet each guest with a smile in your voice as well as on your face**. When a guest is approaching, **you should first establish and keep eye contact with the guest**. Then try to find out the guest's name immediately and use it during the conversation. Always use polite titles as "Mr." or "Ms." **When addressing the guest, do not call a guest by his or her first name**.

Next, find out if the guest has a reservation. Then, check the reservation in the computer and confirm the room information with the guest.

After that, ask the guest to show his or her passport and to fill out the registration form. When the form is ready, you should try to find out the needs of the guest, e.g. the position of the room.

Then, assign a room to the guest and prepare the key to the room. Before

Hotel Check-in   Item 2

giving the key to the guest, **ask the guest to show his or her credit card for an imprint or to pay a deposit.** Upon receiving the credit card, check the name of the cardholder and validity. Collect 150% of the room rate and give the guest the receipt. Next, confirm with the guest the departure date, room rate and other needs. Fill out the room card and tell the guest the room number. If there's nothing wrong, give the guest the room card and key to the room. When everything is done, thank the guest and wish him /her a pleasant stay.

At last, turn in the guest registration form, credit card imprint and a copy of deposit receipt to the cashier.

Task 3

Listen and Answer

You will hear five questions. Listen carefully and give an appropriate answer to each of them.

(1) _____
(2) _____
(3) _____
(4) _____
(5) _____

Task 4

Oral Practice

Retell the text in your own words.

Task 5

More Oral and Listening Practice:
【Listening】 Listen to the dialogs and fill in the blanks.

Listening I

A Group Reservation

R: Receptionist   C: Customer

R: Good morning. Reservations. _____?
C: Good morning. I'd like to _____.

R: What _____?
C: We have 10 people. _____, please.
R: For which dates?
C: From _____ of March.
R: Wait a minute, please. _____ for March _____. Yes, those rooms are _____.
C: What will be the rate?
R: It's _____ per night.
C: Can you give us _____ since we always _____?
R: May I have your name, please?
C: Brutes Lewis from General Traveling Company.
R: Oh, Yes, Mr. Lewis, there is a _____ percent discount for regular customers.
C: How can I _____?
R: You can guarantee the reservation with your _____.
C: My _____ is 3600 54762 5819.
R: OK. Mr. Lewis. How will you be arriving?
C: _____. Do you have _____ service?
R: When will you be arriving at the airport?
C: The arrival time should be _____.
R: OK. Our hotel bus will be there at that time.

Listening II

Extending the Stay

R: Receptionist   G: Guest

R: Good morning, sir. _____ ?
G: I meant to check out today, but I have to _____.
R: May I know your _____?
G: Andrew Stowe of Room _____.
R: Please _____, Mr. Stowe. I'll _____ Here, today is 12th. You _____?
G: Yes, exactly.
R: I'm sorry, sir. You can only stay in that room _____. Your floor was reserved for a conference _____.
G: What will be my _____?
R: Would you mind changing to room _____?
C: Not at all.

Hotel Check-in Item 2

R: Thank you, sir. This is your registration form. Please _____.
G: OK.

【Topics】 Divide the class into groups. Choose one of the following topics to discuss in each group. Give a short report about the group's opinion after that.

1. When you go traveling, what kind of hotel would you prefer? Why?
2. Why do you think teamwork is essential in the running of a good hotel?
3. Comment on the advantages and disadvantages of working as a hotel front desk clerk.

Item 3 Housekeeping Service

客 房 服 务

Model 1:
   Escorting the Guest into the Guest Room
   陪送客人进房

Model 2:
   Making Up the Room   收拾房间

Model 3:
   About Room Service Order   客房用餐服务

Model 4:
   Hotels Today   今日酒店

Housekeeping Service   Item 3

Model 1
Escorting the Guest into the Guest Room　陪送客人进房

Task 1

Warm-up

Work in pairs. Learn the following words about hotel services. Then answer the questions below.

front office	housekeeping	food preparation
F& B service	marketing	accounting

1. What sector of the hotel industry most appeals to you?
2. Think of two positions in each sector.
3. When doing housekeeping service, what should the attendant pay attention to?

Task 2

Learning Points

Listen to the following *words* and *useful expressions* and repeat. Then try to memorize them.

Words and Phrases

usher	['ʌʃə]	v.	引领
spacious	['speisʃəs]	adj.	宽敞的
wardrobe	['wɔ:drəub]	n.	衣柜
faucet	['fɔ:sit]	n.	水龙头
switch	[switʃ]	n.	开关
laptop	['læptɔp]	n.	手提电脑
lobby attendant			大堂服务员
safe-deposit box			保险箱

Useful Expressions

1. Welcome to our floor.
   欢迎光临本楼层。

31

2. I'm the attendant for this floor.
   我是本楼层的服务员。
3. There is a price list over there.
   那里有一个价目单。
4. There is an internet broad band access hookup on the desk.
   桌子上有一个宽带上网接口。
5. If you need any help, please let me know.
   如果您需要帮助，请告知我。

Task 3

Dialogue I

Listen to the *dialogue I* for the first time. Then practise the dialogue by reading it aloud with your partner. Read through it at least twice, changing your role each time.

Escorting the Guest into the Guest Room

【Scene】 *The lobby attendant ushers Mr. Jones onto the floor of his room. The floor attendant, Xiao Hu is waiting for them.*

L: Lobby attendant   X: Xiao Hu   J: Jones

L: Hello, Xiao Hu. This is Mr. Jones of Room 1506.
X: Nice to meet you, Mr. Jones. **Welcome to our floor.**
J: Nice to meet you, too.
X: **I'm the attendant for this floor.** We're glad to have you here. This way, please.
J: Good.
X: Here we are. This is your room, Mr. Jones.
J: Oh, the room seems very spacious!
X: Yes. Mr. Jones, could I put your suitcase by the wardrobe?
J: Yes, please.
X: Well, Mr. Jones, let me introduce the facilities in the room. First, let's see the bathroom. The red faucet is for hot water and the white one is for cold water.
J: Is the water drinkable?
X: No. You may get hot drinking water from the mini-jar, and cold drinks from the mini-bar.
J: Do you have a price list for the things in the mini-bar?
X: Yes, **there is a price list over there.** Well, and this is the air-conditioning switch. The temperature in your room can be adjusted as you like.

Housekeeping Service   Item 3

J: Can I make IDD calls in the room?
X: Yes. For IDD calls, just dial 9, and then 0-0. Next, dial the country code and the area code before the phone number you want to call. Besides, there is a phone index on the desk.
J: I see. Is the Internet available through my laptop?
X: Certainly. **There is an internet broad band access hookup on the desk.**
J: How much do you charge for the use of it?
X: It's 5 RMB per hour. Would you please keep your valuables in the safe-deposit box in the wardrobe?
J: Certainly. Thank you so much.
X: It's my pleasure. **If you need any help, please let me know.**

Task 4

Listen and Answer

You will hear five questions. Listen carefully and give an appropriate answer to each of them.

(1) _____
(2) _____
(3) _____
(4) _____
(5) _____

Task 5

Role-play

Act out the following dialogs.

【Situation A】 The lobby attendant escorts Mr. Johnson to the floor attendant. And the floor attendant escorts Mr. Johnson into his room.

Lobby attendant:
☆ Greets Mr. Johnson.
☆ Introduces Mr. Johnson to the floor attendant.

The floor attendant:
☆ Greets Mr. Johnson and extends welcome to him.
☆ Introduce the basic facilities in the room (bathroom, water, remote control, etc.).
☆ Tells Mr. Johnson that IDD calls could be made after being open.
☆ Tells Mr. Johnson that Internet is available and free of charge.

☆ Tell Mr. Johnson that there are room services for food and drink and that there is a pricelist on the desk.

☆ Tell Mr. Johnson that other helps are available when being told.

Mr. Johnson:

☆ Greets the lobby attendant.
☆ Greets the floor attendant.
☆ Asks whether the IDD calls could be made.
☆ Asks whether Internet is available and how much it is to use it.
☆ Asks whether there are room services for food and drink and the price.
☆ Thanks the floor attendant for the information.

【Situation B】 At the front office, the lobby attendant receives a couple of foreign tourists.

【Situation C】 On a certain floor, the floor attendant escorts a foreign tourist into his room.

Model 2
Making Up the Room 收拾房间

Task 1

Warm-up

Work in pairs. Learn the following words about hotel services. Then answer the questions below.

disturb	towel	toilet
tidy up	turn-down service	

When a room attendant is to make up the room, what should he/she say to the guest?

Task 2

Learning Points

Listen to the following *words* and *useful expressions* and repeat. Then try to memorize them.

Words and Phrases

towel   ['tauəl, taul]   n.   毛巾

Housekeeping Service   Item 3

overnight	[ˈəuvəˈnait]	adv.	通宵
mess	[mes]	n.	混乱
cozy	[ˈkəuzi]	adj.	舒适的，温馨的
turn-down service			做晚床，即整理房间备晚上使用。

Useful Expressions

1. Should I do the turn-down service for you now?
   我现在来做晚床好吗？
2. Would you tidy up a bit in the bathroom?
   请把卫生间收拾一下吧。
3. Would you like me to draw the curtains for you, sir and madam?
   我把窗帘给您拉上好吗？
4. Is there anything else I can do for you?
   还有什么我需要为您服务的？
5. We try to be always at your service.
   我们将尽力为您服务。

Task 3

Dialogue II

Listen to the *dialogue II* for the first time. Then practise the dialogue by reading it aloud with your partner. Read through it at least twice, changing your role each time.

Making up the Room

【Scene】 The Browns are sitting in the room when a room attendant knocks at the door to see whether the turn-down service is to be done.

   A: room attendant   B: Mrs. Brown   C: Mr. Brown

A: Good evening, sir and madam. **Should I do the turn-down service for you now?**

B: Oh, thank you. But we are having some friends over to have a small party here in the room. Could you come back in three hours?

A: Certainly, madam. I'll be off at seven, but I'll let the overnight staff know. They will come then.

B: That's fine. Well, our friends seem to be a little late. **Would you tidy up a bit in the bathroom?**

A: No problem.

B:	Besides, please bring us a bottle of just boiled water. We'd treat our guests with typical Chinese tea.
A:	Yes, madam. I'll bring in some fresh towels together with the drinking water.
B:	OK.
A:	(*Having done all on request*) It's growing dark. **Would you like me to draw the curtains for you, sir and madam?**
B:	Why not? That would be so cozy.
A:	May I turn on the lights for you?
C:	Yes, please. I'd like to read short stories while waiting.
A:	Yes, sir. **Is there anything else I can do for you?**
B:	Nothing more. Thank you very much. You're a smart boy indeed.
A:	**We try to be always at your service.** Good-bye, sir and madam, and do have a very pleasant evening.

Task 4

Listen and Answer

You will hear five questions. Listen carefully and give an appropriate answer to each of them.

(1) _____
(2) _____
(3) _____
(4) _____
(5) _____

Task 5

Role-play

Act out the following dialogs.

【Situation A】 A room attendant who is to make up the room for a foreign guest. They are having a conversation in the guest's room.

Room attendant:
☆ (knocks at the door) Asks whether it is convenient to make up the room right now.
☆ Asks what is the proper time to come again.
☆ Comes at 3:00 and asks to come in for the room service.
☆ Finishes the room service and asks whether to draw the curtain.

Housekeeping Service　　Item 3

- ☆ Asks whether other services are needed.
- ☆ Brings some boiled water and wishes good night.

Guest:
- ☆ Tells the room attendant to come later.
- ☆ Tells the room attendant to come at 3:00.
- ☆ Gives permission.
- ☆ Says that he will do that by himself.
- ☆ Asks for some boiled water.
- ☆ Expresses thanks and says good-bye.

【Situation B】 Suppose you are a room attendant, consider the following questions and imagine what you will say before, during and after the room service. Discuss with your partner, and then speak it by yourself.

(1) Ask whether it is convenient for you to make up the room right now.
(2) If you get a negative answer, ask what time would be convenient for you to come back.
(3) When you finish making up the room, ask whether other services are needed.
(4) If the guests complain about the delay of the room service, try to give a satisfying explanation.

Model 3
About Room Service Order　客房用餐服务

Task 1

Warm-up

Work in pairs. If you are a room attendant, how do you introduce the items of room service to the guests? Discuss with your partner.

Task 2

Learning Points

Listen to the following *words* and *useful expressions* and repeat. Then try to memorize them.

Words and Phrases

croissant	[krwəː'sɑːnt]	n.	羊角面包
donut	['dəuˌnʌt]	n.	炸面圈
pot	[pɔt]	n.	罐，壶
extra	['ekstrə]	adv./ adj.	另外的，额外的
salad	['sæləd]	n.	色拉
room service			（客房）用餐服务

Useful Expressions

1. What would you like to order?
   您想点些什么？
2. Would you like a cup of coffee or a pot of coffee?
   您是要一杯咖啡还是要一壶咖啡？
3. A pot costs about 20 RMB extra.
   一壶要多花二十元钱。
4. Our waiter will be there in around 10 minutes.
   服务生大约分钟后给您送去。
5. Please feel free to ask.
   请尽管讲。

Task 3

Dialogue III

Listen to the *dialogue III* for the first time. Then practise the dialogue by reading it aloud with your partner. Read through it at least twice, changing your role each time.

About Room Service Order

【Scene】 *Mr. Lock in Room 1608 orders his breakfast. The staff takes his order.*

S: staff   L: Mr. Lock

S: Good morning. Room service. What can I do for you?
L: Hi, I'd like to order some food for my breakfast.
S: Yes, sir. **What would you like to order?**
L: I'd like a ham and cheese croissant, a boiled egg, and a coffee.
S: **Would you like a cup of coffee or a pot of coffee?**
L: What's the difference?
S: **A pot costs about 20 RMB extra.**

Housekeeping Service   Item 3

L: A pot please.
S: Anything else?
L: Do you have green salads?
S: Yes, sir. Do you want one?
L: Yes, a green salad.
S: Anything else?
L: No, that's all.
S: Could I have your name?
L: Mr. Lock of Room 1608.
S: So, Mr. Lock, we'll send to Room 1608 one ham and cheese croissant, a boiled egg, a pot of coffee and a green salad. **Our waiter will be there in around 10 minutes.** If there is anything more you may need, **please feel free to ask.**
L: OK.
S: Thank you. I hope you'll have a good day.

Task 4

Listen and Answer

You will hear five questions. Listen carefully and give an appropriate answer to each of them.

(1) _____
(2) _____
(3) _____
(4) _____
(5) _____

Task 5

Role-play

Act out the following dialogs.

【Situation A】 A guest (Mr. Jerry) of room 2135 orders some fruit through room service. The staff of room service answers the phone call.

The staff:
☆ Answers the phone and offers help.
☆ Says that fruit orders can be made and asks what to order.
☆ Confirms the kinds and amounts of the fruit and asks if anything more.
☆ Asks the brand of the beer.

- ☆ Asks the room and name of the guest.
- ☆ Tells the guest to wait for about half an hour.

Mr. Jerry:
- ☆ Asks whether fruit can be ordered.
- ☆ Orders some fruit for a small party.
- ☆ Orders 3 kilos bananas, 3 kilos of apples, 2 kilos of grapes, one kilo of strawberries.
- ☆ Tells the staff to buy a box of the most popular local beer.
- ☆ Tells the name and room.
- ☆ Expresses thanks.

【Situation B】A guest orders supper for his wife and himself, the staff of the room service answers the phone.

Model 4
Hotels Today 今日酒店

Task 1

Learning Points

Listen to the following *words* and *useful expressions* and repeat. Then try to memorize it.

Words and Phrases

generally	[ˈdʒenərəli]	adv.	一般，通常
vacation	[vəˈkeiʃən; veiˈkeiʃən]	n.	假期，度假
commercial	[kəˈməːʃəl]	adj.	商业的
transient	[ˈtrænziənt]	adj.	短暂的，瞬时的
resort	[riˈzɔːt]	n.	胜地
seashore	[ˈsiːʃɔː]	n.	海岸，海滨
residential	[ˌreziˈdenʃəl]	adj.	住宅的，与居住有关的
luxurious	[lʌɡˈzjuəriəs]	adj.	奢侈的，豪华的
inexpensive	[ˌiniksˈpensiv]	adj.	便宜的，不贵的
range	[reindʒ]	n.	范围，行列
moderate	[ˈmɔdərit]	adj.	中等的，适度的

Housekeeping Service   Item 3

Useful Expressions

1. Hotels designed for business people are known as commercial or transient hotels.
   为出差人士设计的酒店被称为商业酒店。
2. Transient hotels are usually located in the business section of town.
   商业酒店常建在城市的商业区。
3. This (residential) is designed to meet the needs of people who want to live in a hotel.
   这种（居家）酒店是为了满足那些想长住在酒店的人们的需要。
4. Some hotels have as few as ten rooms, and others have several hundred.
   一些酒店只有十来间房，一些酒店有数百间房。
5. Hotels range from the very luxurious, which charge high rates, to the small and inexpensive that fall within the price range of large number of travelers.
   酒店等次不同，豪华的收费很高，小的酒店和便宜的酒店能把价钱定得使大批的旅客能够接受。

Task 2

Passage Reading

Listen to the short passage for the first time. Then practise it by reading them aloud by yourself.

Hotels Today

Hotels today are quite different from those of the past. People who stay in them are generally traveling for business, or they are touring or on vacation. So hotels are designed mainly to meet the needs of one of those two groups of people. **Hotels designed for business people are known as commercial or transient hotels.** Hotels for people on vacation are called vacation or resort hotels.

Transient hotels are usually located in the business section of town, while resort hotels may be at the seashore, on a mountain lake, or in the desert.

In addition to these two main types, there is a third type of hotel, called a residential hotel. **This is designed to meet the needs of people who want to live in a hotel.** Inns and hotels are located in nearly every population center in the world. In the United States alone there are about thirty thousand. **Some hotels have as few as ten rooms, and others have several hundred.** Among the largest hotels in the world today are the Conrad Hilton in Chicago, Illinois, and the Russia in Moscow, each with about three thousand rooms. In every hotel, travelers find small single rooms for the use of one person; larger double rooms for the use of two people and arrangement of two or more rooms, called suites, which can be used by a group of persons traveling together.

Hotels range from the very luxurious, which charge high rates, to the small and inexpensive that fall within the price range of large number of travelers. The price for a suite of rooms in a luxury hotel may be $50 a day and up, while a double room in a moderate-price hotel may cost $8 or $10 a day and up.

Task 3

Listen and Answer

You will hear five questions. Listen carefully and give an appropriate answer to each of them.

(1) _____
(2) _____
(3) _____
(4) _____
(5) _____

Task 4

Oral Practice

Retell the text in your own words.

Task 5

More Oral and Listening Practice:
【Listening】 Listen to the dialogs and fill in the blanks.

Listening I

A Morning Call

A:　Can I help you, sir?
B:　It's _____ here. Do you have _____ service?
A:　Yes, would you like to have it?
B:　Yes, I want to _____ tomorrow morning.

Housekeeping Service   Item 3

A: _____ do you want to have it?
B: At_____ tomorrow morning. I want to get up early so that I can _____.
A: Oh, I see. What kind of call would you like, by _____ or by _____?
B: By phone, I don't like to disturb _____.
A: Your room number, please.
B: _____.
A: OK, sir. Our _____ will do that for you

Listening II

Cleaning the Room

A: Housekeeping. May I _____?
B: Yes, please.
A: Good morning, sir. May I _____?
B: No, _____. Thanks. I'm not feeling very well now. I've _____.
A: Oh, I'm sorry_____. Shall I _____?
B: Not necessary. I've got some medicine.
A: Would _____?
B: Yes, please switch on the mini-jar to make me some boiled water.
A: Yes, sir. May I replace the _____?
B: That's very kind of you.
A: Should I turn on the _____ light?
B: Yes, please. I _____.

【Topics】 Divide the class into groups. Choose one of the following topics to discuss in each group. Give a short report about the group's opinion after that.

1. Do you agree to the saying "A hotel is a highly organized commercial unit." ? Why or why not?
2. In the past twenty years or so, a large number of five star hotels have been built in China. Comment on this phenomenon.
3. When you go traveling, what kind of hotel would you prefer? Why?

Item 4 Food & Beverage Service

餐 饮 服 务

Model 1:
　　Reserving a Table　预定餐桌

Model 2:
　　Helping to Order Dishes　帮助点菜

Model 3:
　　The Payment　付款

Model 4:
　　The Chinese Food　中国饮食

Food & Beverage Service   Item 4

Model 1
Reserving a Table 预定餐桌

Task 1

Warm-up

Work in pairs. Learn the following words of the sectors of food and beverage services. Then answer the questions below.

| fry | simmer | bake | roast | stew | cocktail | wine |
| liquor | spirits | juice | oven | wok | pot | |

1. What kind of food and drink do you usually have at home?
2. Say something about the way of cooking you know.
3. Do you know the different utensils or appliance used in cooking?

Task 2

Learning Points

Listen to the following *words* and *useful expressions* and repeat. Then try to memorize them.

Words and Phrases

waitress	['weitris]	n.	女服务员
era	['iərə]	n.	时代，年代
vacant	['veikənt]	adj.	空的
come over			来，过来
view of the street			街景
dress code			着装标准
look forward to (doing)			期望，盼望

Useful Expressions

1. I want to reserve a table in your restaurant.
   我想在你们饭店订张桌子。

45

2. For lunch or for supper?
   订中餐还是订晚餐?
3. What time would you come over?
   你们几点来?
4. How many of you would come?
   请问你们几个人?
5. We're looking forward to seeing you.
   我们盼着您的到来。

Task 3

Dialogue I

Listen to the *dialogue I* for the first time. Then practise the dialogue by reading it aloud with your partner. Read through it at least twice, changing your role each time.

Reserving a Table

【Scene】 *A waitress in a restaurant receives a telephone call from a customer to book a table for lunch.*

W: Waitress   C: Customer

W: Good morning. New Era Restaurant. Can I help you?
C: **I want to reserve a table in your restaurant.**
W: **For lunch or for supper?**
C: For lunch.
W: **What time would you come over?**
C: We'll arrive at around 11:30.
W: **How many of you would come, sir?**
C: We are a group of 10.
W: OK. Could I have your name, please?
C: Frank Chen.
W: We have two vacant rooms now, 306 and 502. Which one do you prefer?
C: 502, Please. We want to have a view of the street.
W: Ok. Mr. Chen, you'll have a table of 10 at 502 for lunch. Do you have any dress code?
C: No. Thank you.
W: My pleasure. **We're looking forward to seeing you.**

Food & Beverage Service   Item 4

Task 4

Listen and Answer

You will hear five questions. Listen carefully and give an appropriate answer to each of them.

(1) _____
(2) _____
(3) _____
(4) _____
(5) _____

Task 5

Role-play

Act out the following dialogs.

【Situation A】 The headwaiter of Rainbow Restaurant is receiving a telephone call from a customer to book a table. Please make a conversation with the clues offered below.

The headwaiter:
☆ Greets and tells the name of the restaurant and offers help.
☆ Asks the time the customer want to reserve.
☆ Asks the number of the people of the reserved table.
☆ Asks the customer to have smoking or non-smoking area.
☆ Asks whether there is a dress code.
☆ Asks the name of the customer.
☆ Expresses wish to see the customer.

The customer:
☆ Asks to reserve a table.
☆ Tells the headwaiter to reserve a table for supper.
☆ Says that there are seven adults.
☆ Says to have non-smoking area.
☆ Tells the headwaiter there's no dress code.
☆ Tells the name.
☆ Expresses thanks.

【Situation B】 The staff of the Diamond restaurant receives a telephone call to reserve a table for 7:00. But there is no vacant table at that time. So he asks the customer whether he would reserve a table for 8:00. The customer gives a positive reply.

Model 2
Helping to Order Dishes 帮助点菜

Task 1

Warm-up

Work in pairs. Learn the following words and answer the questions below.

chicken	duck	mutton	beef	seafood	fish
tomato	potato	greens		bamboo shoots	pickles

What kind of food do you like to have in a restaurant?

Task 2

Learning Points

Listen to the following *words* and *useful expressions* and repeat. Then try to memorize them.

Words and Phrases

bewilder	[bi'wildə]	v.	使迷惑，使不知所措
recommend	[rekə'mend]	v.	推荐
chef	[ʃef]	n.	厨师
steam	[stiːm]	v.	蒸
shad	[ʃæd]	n.	西鲱，鲥鱼
crispy	['krispi]	adj.	脆的
stew	[stjuː]	v.	炖，焖
chestnuts	['tʃestnʌt]	n.	栗子
mushroom	['mʌʃrum]	n.	蘑菇
cabbage	['kæbidʒ]	n.	甘蓝，卷心菜
brandy	['brændi]	n.	白兰地酒

Useful Expressions

1. Would you like me to recommend something?
   要不要我帮您推荐几个？

Food & Beverage Service   Item 4

2. Today's recommendation by our chef is steamed shad.
   今天厨师推荐菜是清蒸鲥鱼。
3. How about shrimps with crispy fried rice?
   虾仁锅巴怎么样?
4. What else do you want to have?
   别的还要点什么?
5. Stewed chicken with chestnuts is another special dish here.
   板栗炖鸡是我们的另一个特色菜。
6. Winter mushrooms with green cabbage are worth trying too.
   冬菇卷心菜也值得一尝。
7. Please wait for a short while.
   请稍等。

Task 3

Dialogue II

Listen to the *dialogue II* for the first time. Then practise the dialogue by reading it aloud with your partner. Read through it at least twice, changing your role each time.

Helping to Order Dishes

【Scene】 *The waiter gives the menu to Mr. Hans and waits for a moment to take the order. Mr. Hans seems a little bewildered with the menu.*

W: the waiter   H: Mr. Hans

W: Excuse me, sir. **Would you like me to recommend something**?
H: Oh, yes. There are so many good-looking dishes on the menu. I really don't know what to order.
W: **Today's recommendation by our chef is steamed shad.**
H: Oh, but I don't like fish of any kind. Do you have any other things to recommend?
W: Well, **how about shrimps with crispy fried rice,** (pointing at the picture) here?
H: That sounds good.
W: **What else do you want to have,** beef, chicken or duck?
H: What do you recommend?
W: **Stewed chicken with chestnuts is another special dish here.**
H: I'd like to have it.
W: **Winter mushrooms with green cabbage are worth trying too.**

H: Yes, I need to have some vegetables.
W: Anything to drink, sir?
H: I'll have brandy.
W: Ok, sir. Is that all?
H: I guess it's enough, isn't it?
W: Yes, sir. Thank you. **Please wait for a short while**.

Task 4

Listen and Answer

You will hear five questions. Listen carefully and give an appropriate answer to each of them.

(1) _____
(2) _____
(3) _____
(4) _____
(5) _____

Task 5

Role-play

Act out the following dialogs.

【Situation A】 A foreign guest in a Chinese restaurant does not know what to order. The waiter comes up to help him.

The waiter:
☆ Asks what kind of food he wants to have.
☆ Recommends one or two dishes in the restaurant.
☆ Asks the guest what else to order.
☆ Recommend several kinds of vegetables (lettuce, spinach, romaine, snake gourd, asparagus).
☆ Asks whether to have some drink.
☆ Asks whether to have something else.
☆ Thanks the guest and takes the order.

The guest:
☆ Asks for the help to order dishes.
☆ Asks whether they have something special.
☆ Orders the dish recommended.

Food & Beverage Service　　Item 4

☆ Asks the waiter to recommend some vegetable.
☆ Chooses one kind of the vegetable recommended.
☆ Orders some wine.
☆ Tells the waiter to order nothing more.

【Situation B】 Choose one of the dishes that you are familiar with to discuss and describe how it is made. Suppose your partner is a foreign guest. Make a conversation to explain the method of making the dish.

Model 3
The Payment　付款

Task 1

Warm-up

Work in pairs. If you are the waiter to collect the bill, what questions would you usually ask?

Task 2

Learning Points

Listen to the following *words* and *useful expressions* and repeat. Then try to memorize them.

Words and Phrases

total	['təutl]	n.	总额
cashier	[kə'ʃiə]	n.	出纳，收银员
honor	['ɔnə]	v.	接受信用卡付款
password	['pɑːswəːd]	n.	密码
sign	[sain]	v.	签名
credit card			信用卡
exchange rate			汇率
Visa			一种信用卡，音译为"维萨"等不同译法
American Express			美国运通卡

Useful Expressions

1. The total is 182 RMB.
   总共是182元人民币。
2. How much is it in dollars?
   合多少美元？
3. I'll ask the cashier.
   我问一下收银员。
4. It's 26 dollars at today's exchange rate.
   按今天的汇率是26美元。
5. Do you honor credit cards?
   你们是否接受信用卡付款？
6. What kind of card have you got?
   您是什么卡？
7. Would you please come over to put in the password?
   请过来输下密码好吗？
8. Please sign your name here.
   请在这儿签名。

Task 3

Dialogue III

Listen to the *dialogue III* for the first time. Then practise the dialogue by reading it aloud with your partner. Read through it at least twice, changing your role each time.

The Payment

【Scene】*A foreign customer is paying at a restaurant and the waiter brings the bill.*

C: customer   W: waiter

C: Waiter, may I have the bill?
W: Yes, sir. Here it is.
C: How much is it?
W: **The total is 182 RMB.**
C: Do you accept US dollars?
W: Yes, sir.
C: **How much is it in dollars?**
W: A moment please, **I'll ask the cashier. It's 26 dollars at today's**

Food & Beverage Service   Item 4

exchange rate.
C: **Do you honor credit cards?**
W: Yes. **What kind of card have you got, sir?**
C: I have Visa and American Express, which do you prefer?
W: Both are OK. It's up to you. **Would you please come over to put in the password?**
C: Oh, yes.
W: Thank you. **Please sign your name here.**
C: OK.
W: Thank you.

Task 4

Listen and Answer

You will hear five questions. Listen carefully and give an appropriate answer to each of them.
(1) _____
(2) _____
(3) _____
(4) _____
(5) _____

Task 5

Role-play

Act out the following dialogs.

【Situation A】 A customer in the restaurant wants to buy the bill. Make a conversation with the clues below:

The customer:
☆ Asks the waiter to come over with the bill.
☆ Asks the total of the bill.
☆ Asks whether the restaurant accepts an American Express.
☆ Asks whether the restaurant accepts a Visa Card.
☆ Asks whether the bill can be put on the hotel bill.
☆ Tells the waiter of the room number.

The waiter:
☆ Brings the bill and gives it to the customer.

- ☆ Confirms the total of the bill.
- ☆ Tells the customer the restaurant does not accept American Express.
- ☆ Tells the customer that a Visa Card is not accepted either.
- ☆ Says that the bill can be put on the hotel bill and asks the room number of the customer.
- ☆ Thanks the customer and wishes him good night.

【Situation B】A foreigner in the restaurant wants to buy the bill. He only has credit cards, traveler's checks and foreign currency, while the restaurant only accepts RMB or credits cards issued in China. Suppose you are the waiter, what will you do?

Model 4
The Chinese Food 中国饮食

Task 1

Learning Points

Listen to the following *words* and *useful expressions* and repeat. Then try to memorize them.

Words and Phrases

varied	['vɛərid]	*adj.*	各种各样的
complex	['kɔmpleks]	*adj.*	复杂的
culinary	['kʌlinəri]	*adj.*	厨房的，烹调的
appreciation	[ə,pri:ʃi'eiʃən]	*n.*	欣赏
flavor	['fleivə]	*n.*	味道
geographical	[,dʒiə'græfikəl]	*adj.*	地理的，地域的
hot	[hɔt]	*adj.*	热的，辣的
salty	['sɔ:lti]	*adj.*	咸的
sour	['sauə]	*adj.*	酸的
dispute	[dis'pju:t]	*n.*	争议
pungent	['pʌndʒənt]	*adj.*	刺激的，辛辣的
greasy	['gri:si, 'gri:zi]	*adj.*	油腻的
tender	['tendə]	*adj.*	嫩的
average	['ævəridʒ]	*adj.*	普通的

composition	[kɔmpəˈziʃən]	n.	构成，组成
consume	[kənˈsjuːm]	v.	消费，吃
accompany	[əˈkʌmpəni]	n.	伴随
calory	[kæləri]	n.	卡路里（热量单位）
grain	[grein]	n.	谷物，粮食
according to			根据
vary from to…			从……到……不等，在……到……之间
be characterized with			以……为特征

Useful Expressions

1. Great attention is paid to culinary appreciation of the food because the food should be good not only in flavor and smell, but also in color and appearance.
   人们非常注重菜肴的观赏性,不仅要求它香、味俱佳,还要色泽、外表好看。

2. Chinese food varies from place to place mainly according to geographical difference.
   中国菜肴主要是因地域不同而不同。

3. The exact number of regional cuisine is still under dispute.
   地方菜系的确切数目还存在争议。

4. Huaiyang cuisine is characterized by its sweet flavor.
   淮扬菜的特点是甜。

5. For most Chinese, about 65 percent of an average meal's calories come from grain sources instead of meat or vegetable dishes.
   对于大多数中国人而言，普通饭菜65%的热量是来自米面而不是肉类和蔬菜。

Task 2

Passage Reading

Listen to the short passage for the first time. Then practise it by reading it aloud by yourself.

The Chinese Food

Four words are often used to describe Chinese food. They are "colorful", "varied", "delicious" and "complex". **Great attention is paid to culinary appreciation of the food because the food should be good not only in flavor and smell, but also in color and appearance.**

Chinese food varies from place to place mainly according to geographical difference. Some dishes are hot, some sweet, some are salty and others sour. **The exact number of regional cuisine is still under dispute,** but experts agree on at least four: Sichuan, Shandong, Cantonese, and Huaiyang. Of each cuisine, there are several types. For instance, the Shandong cuisine includes Beijing food and Shandong food. Sichuan cuisine is characterized by its hot and pungent flavoring. The features of Shandong cuisine are fresh, tasty and not greasy. Cantonese cuisine is known for its fresh, tender and lightly seasoned flavor. **Huaiyang cuisine is characterized by its sweet flavor.**

However, an average Chinese meal at home is quite different in composition from a Chinese banquet. At an everyday home meal, an adult may consume two small bowls of steamed rice, or a large bowl of noodles, or several pieces of steamed bread, accompanied by several meat or vegetable dished, but not the other way round. **For most Chinese, about 65 percent of an average meal's calories come from grain sources instead of meat or vegetable dishes.**

Task 3

Listen and Answer

You will hear five questions. Listen carefully and give an appropriate answer to each of them.

(1) _____
(2) _____
(3) _____
(4) _____
(5) _____

Task 4

Oral Practice

Retell the text in your own words.

Task 5

More Oral and Listening Practice:
【Listening】 Listen to the dialogs and fill in the blanks.

Food & Beverage Service   Item 4

Listening I

Breakfast

W: Waiter   M: Mrs. Black

- **W₁:** Good morning sir and madam. What would you like to have?
- **M:** _____ for breakfast?
- **W₁:** We serve _____ and _____ breakfast.
- **M:** What do you serve for _____ breakfast?
- **W₁:** We serve rolls with _____.
- **M:** What about _____ breakfast?
- **W₁:** Orange or _____ juice, tea or _____, toast with butter or jam, _____ with bacon.
- **W₂:** I'll have _____ juice, _____ and two eggs. Can I have _____ instead of bacon?
- **W₁:** Certainly, madam. And you, sir?
- **M:** I'll have _____ of my wife.

Listening II

At a Chinese Restaurant

W: Waiter   G: Guest

- **W:** Good evening, sir. Can I help you?
- **G:** I'd like to _____, but I _____ about Chinese food. Can you give me some suggestion?
- **W:** Well, there are different _____.
- **G:** Can you give me _____?
- **W:** Four styles of food are especially known throughout China. They are Shandong, Cantonese, Sichuan, and Huaiyang.
- **G:** What is the Cantonese food _____?
- **W:** It is _____.
- **G:** How about Shandong food?
- **W:** It's _____.
- **G:** And what about the Huaiyang food?
- **W:** It's _____.
- **G:** The last one, Sichuan food is?
- **W:** Sichuan dishes are _____.
- **G:** Oh, really. I like hot food. _____?

57

W: The famous Sichuan dishes are Mapo bean curd and shredded meat in chili sauce.

G: I'll _____.

【Topics】 Divide the class into groups. Choose one of the following topics to discuss in each group. Give a short report about the group's opinion after that.

1. Compare the main differences between Chinese food and Western food.
2. Why is Chinese food sold abroad different from the real Chinese food in China?
3. With the society developing rapidly, people's demands for hotel services are changing. If you were a hotel manager, what other services could you offer the guests?

Item 5　City Sightseeing and Transportation

都市观光和交通

Model 1:
　　City Tours　都市游

Model 2:
　　Car Rental Service　租车服务

Model 3:
　　Xikou of Fenghua　奉化溪口

Model 1
City Tours 都市游

Task 1

Warm-up

Work in pairs. Answer the questions below.

1. Shanghai is one of the most famous cities in China. Have you been to Shanghai? Which attractions impress you most?
2. Can you translate the following scenic spots into Chinese?

the Bund	the Temple of Confucius	the Dianshan Lake scenic Site
the Guyi Garden	Huangpu river Cruise	the Jade Buddha Temple
the Yuyuan Garden	Pudong New District	the Oriental Pearl Tower

Task 2

Learning Points

Listen to the following *words* and *useful expressions* and repeat. Then try to memorize them.

Words and Phrases

fame	[feim]	n.	名声，声誉
deserve	[di'zə:v]	v.	值得
architectural	[,ɑ:ki'tektʃərəl]	adj.	建筑的
exhibition	[,eksi'biʃən]	n.	表现，显示
gorgeous	['gɔ:dʒəs]	adj.	极好的，吸引人的
harmony	['hɑ:məni]	n.	融洽，协调
consulate	['kɔnsjulit]	n.	领事馆
gather	['gæðə]	v.	聚集，集拢
headquarters	['hed,kwɔ:təz]	n. (pl)	(pl) 总部
financial	[fai'nænʃəl, fi-]	adj.	金融的，财政的
institution	[,insti'tju:ʃən]	n.	机构
shabby	['ʃæbi]	adj.	破旧的

City Sightseeing and Transportation　　Item 5

chest-high	adj.	齐胸高的
explicit　[iks'plisit]	adj.	明了的，不言而喻的
the Bund		（上海）外滩
Oriental Manhattan		东方曼哈顿
sightseeing spot		观光点
flood-prevention wall		防汛墙
sightseers' wall		观光墙
go on a cruise		乘游艇游览
on board		上船

Useful Expressions

1. It looks like that fame is well deserved.
   名不虚传。
2. They are known as the " Exhibition of World Architectures ".
   它们以"万国建筑园"而闻名。
3. The place we are standing now is the newly built flood-prevention wall.
   我们现在所站的地方就是新建成的防汛墙。
4. But the newly built sightseers' wall is wider than ever and one can enjoy broader sight.
   但是新建的观光墙比以前更宽，视野也更宽阔。
5. People say it's like a bright pearl on the Huangpu River.
   人们说它像黄浦江上一颗璀璨的明珠。
6. You can say that again!
   你说的对极了！
7. Please on board, everybody!
   请大家上船！

Task 3

Dialogue I

Listen to the *dialogue I* for the first time. Then practise the dialogue by reading it aloud with your partner. Read through it at least twice, changing your role each time.

City Tours

【Scene】 *A tour group from USA is visiting the Bund of Shanghai. The guide is talking about the Bund with the tourists.*

　　　　　　　　　　G: guide　　T: tourist

T:　　This is my first trip to Shanghai, but I heard a long time ago that shanghai was "Oriental Manhattan", and **it looks like that fame is well deserved.** Mingbuxuchuan.

G: Wow, your Chinese is so good!

T: You're too kind. Hey, these houses are really pretty! They don't look like Chinese buildings.

G: Many people say so. These buildings have different European architectural styles. **They are known as the " Exhibition of World Architectures ".**

T: They're gorgeous and in harmony with each other. Who built these buildings?

G: In the past, many foreign countries set up their consulates in this area. And the Bund also gathered the headquarters of international financial institutions in China.

T: What's that? Is it the famous Bund?

G: Yes, you're quite right. Here we are at the Bund, the most famous sightseeing spot in Shanghai. **The place we are standing now is the newly built flood-prevention wall.** Do you know what is used to be?

T: We have no idea.

G: Here used to be a shabby chest-high brick wall called the "Lovers' Wall" along the Huangpu River. The meaning is quite explicit, I think.

T: What a romantic place it was!

G: **But the newly built sightseers' wall is wider than ever and one can enjoy broader sight.** Please turn your eyes across the river. Can you see the tower with bright "pearls"?

T: Yes, is that the TV tower? What's the name of it?

G: The Oriental Pearl TV Tower. **People say it's like a bright pearl on the Huangpu River.** It is 450 meters high and boasts the tallest in Asia, and is a new attraction in Shanghai.

T: What a sight the Bund is!

G: **You can say that again!** Now, ladies and gentlemen, time for us to go on a cruise on the Huangpu River. **Please on board, everybody!**

Task 4

Listen and Answer

You will hear five questions. Listen carefully and give an appropriate answer to each of them.

(1) _____

(2) _____

(3) _____

City Sightseeing and Transportation   Item 5

(4) _____

(5) _____

Task 5

Role-play

Act out the following dialogs.

【Situation A】 John is enjoying the beautiful scenes around the Bund. The guide makes explanations.

The guide:
- ☆ Greets the tourists.
- ☆ Introduces the buildings of European architectural styles.
- ☆ Explains the builder.
- ☆ Introduces the history of the Bund.
- ☆ Explains the Oriental Pearl TV Tower to tourists.
- ☆ Tells tourists to go on a cruise on the Huangpu River.

John:
- ☆ Says that it's the first time visiting Shanghai and knows its famous fame--- Oriental Manhattan.
- ☆ Wants to know that who built these buildings.
- ☆ Wants to know the history of the Bund.
- ☆ Appreciates the fascinating scenes.
- ☆ Wants to know the name of TV tower.
- ☆ Appreciates the Bund.

【Situation B】 Suppose you are now showing your foreign tourists around your hometown and you are telling them something about the famous scenic spots and the traditional Chinese culture in your hometown.

Model 2
Car Rental Service 租车服务

Task 1

Warm-up

Work in pairs. Match the best meaning given below with the expressions that follow and talk about the advantages of the following modes of transport.

| taxi | limousine | shuttle bus | train |
| flight | metro | light rail | maglev train |

1. A plaSne making a particular journey.
2. An above-ground train system.
3. A train that floats about 10mm above the guide way on a magnetic field. It is pulled by the guide way itself by changing magnetic fields.
4. A bus service that goes regularly between two places.
5. A number of connected carriages pulled by an engine along a railway line.
6. A big expensive comfortable car.
7. A car and driver that you pay to take you somewhere.
8. A railway system that runs under the ground below a city.

Task 2

Learning Points

Listen to the following *words* and *useful expressions* and repeat. Then try to memorize them.

Words and Phrases

rent	[rent]	v.	出租，租用
activity	[æk'tiviti]	n.	活动
rental	['rentl]	n.	租赁
available	[ə'veiləbl]	adj.	可用的，有效的
chain	[tʃein]	n.	连锁
procedure	[prə'siːdʒə]	n.	手续
license	['laisəns]	n.	执照
validity	[və'liditi]	n.	有效性，正确性
passport	['pɑːspɔːt]	n.	护照
visa	['viːzə]	n.	签证
guarantor	[ˌgærən'tɔː, gə'ræntɔː]	n.	担保人
stable	['steibl]	adj.	稳定的
career	[kə'riə]	n.	职业
relative	['relətiv]	n.	亲戚
Santana		n.	桑塔纳（汽车）
Passat		n.	帕萨特（汽车）
Buick		n.	别克（汽车）

City Sightseeing and Transportation   Item 5

Honda	['hɔndə]	n.	本田（汽车）
Toyota	['təʊjəʊtə]	n.	丰田（汽车）
BMW		n.	宝马（汽车）
Lincoln	[liŋ'kən]	n.	林肯（汽车）
Rolls Royce		n.	劳斯莱斯（汽车）
deposit	[di'pɔzit]	n.	存款，定金
charge for			索价(要价)
depend on			依赖，依靠，取决于

Useful Expressions

1. Car rental service is available in large cities like Beijing and Shanghai nowadays.
   现在像北京和上海这样的大城市里都有租车服务。
2. You have to have an international driver's license.
   你得要持有国际驾照。
3. They would check the validity of your passport and visa.
   他们要核实你护照和签证的有效期。
4. Last but not least…
   最后，也是很要紧的是……
5. And how much do they usually charge for a day?
   每天的收费是多少？
6. What types do they provide?
   他们都有些什么车？
7. Shall I pay some deposit for the car?
   租车是不是要付定金？

Task 3

Dialogue II

Listen to the *dialogue II* for the first time. Then practise the dialogue by reading it aloud with your partner. Read through it at least twice, changing your role each time.

Car Rental Service

【Scene】 *A tourist wants to rent a car for his daily activities. The guide is telling him how to use the car rental service in the city.*

G: guide   T: tourist

G: Good morning, sir. May I help you?

T: I'll have a lot of business to do while I'm here. So, do you think it possible for me to rent a car for myself?

G: Yes. **Car rental service is available in large cities like Beijing and Shanghai nowadays.**

T: Really? Where and how is the service offered?

G: Well, I know some car rental companies in the city, most of which are chains.

T: That's fine. What would be the procedure?

G: Well, first of all, **you have to have an international driver's license.**

T: Luckily, I've got one with me.

G: Fine. Second, **they would check the validity of your passport and visa.**

T: My visa is valid until 2007.

G: OK. **Last but not least,** a local guarantor is required, who must have a stable career and income.

T: That might be a problem. I have neither friends nor relatives here. I wonder if you…

G: Aha, you want me to be your guarantor? OK, that shouldn't be a problem.

T: Thank you very much! **And how much do they usually charge for a day?**

G: Something between 200 to 400 yuan RMB, depending on the type of car you rent.

T: **What types do they provide?**

G: Quite a lot. The Chinese Santana, Passat and Buick, the Japanese Toyota, Honda, the German BMW, the American Lincoln and Ford, the French and British Rolls Royce, and so on.

T: That's very kind of you. By the way, **shall I pay some deposit for the car?**

G: Sure. About $ 1000.

Task 4

Listen and Answer

You will hear five questions. Listen carefully and give an appropriate answer to each of them.

(1) _____

(2) _____

(3) _____

City Sightseeing and Transportation   Item 5

(4) _____
(5) _____

Task 5

Role-play

Act out the following dialogs.

【Situation A】 You are a guide and your tourist wants to rent a car to travel by herself. Make a short dialogue with your partner on the topic of "Car Rental Service".

The guide:
☆ Greets the tourist and asks what she wants to help.
☆ Tells the procedure of renting a car: driving experience and international driver's license available, validity of passport and visa and a local guarantor.
☆ Tells the charge of car rental.
☆ Tells all the types of car provided in the car rental company.
☆ Tells how much deposit should be paid.

The tourist:
☆ Tells the reason for renting a car.
☆ Asks the charge of car rental.
☆ Asks the types of car provided.
☆ Asks whether pay some deposit for the car.

【Situation B】 Now you are at Hangzhou and want to visit the scenic spots by bike. So you have to hire a bike.

Model 3
Xikou of Fenghua　奉化溪口

Task 1

Learning Points

Listen to the following *words* and *useful expressions* and repeat. Then try to memorize them.

Words and Phrases

population	[ˌpɔpju'leiʃən]	n.	人口
administrative	[əd'ministrətiv]	adj.	行政的，管理的
residence	['rezidəns]	n.	住处，住宅
construction	[kən'strʌkʃən]	n.	建设，建造
consist	[kən'sist]	v.	组成
wing	[wiŋ]	n.	翅膀，翼
corridor	['kɔridɔ:]	n.	走廊
traditional	[trə'diʃən(ə)l]	adj.	传统的
aristocratic	[ˌæristə'krætik]	adj.	贵族的，贵族气派的
decoration	[ˌdekə'reiʃən]	n.	装饰，装饰品
application	[ˌæpli'keiʃən]	n.	应用
temperament	['tempərəmənt]	n.	气质，性质，性情
Chiang Kai-shek			蒋介石
four-A state-level			4A 级
human culture			人文景观
natural scene			自然景观
lower street			下街
Shan Stream			剡溪
Bijia Hill			笔架山

Useful Expressions

1. Its human culture and natural scene are famous both at home and abroad.
   景区内人文景观、自然景观名震海内外。
2. It is located at lower street of Wuling Road in Xikou.
   它位于溪口武岭路下街。
3. In front of the house is Shan Stream which is flowing by all the year.
   房前是终年长流不息的剡溪。
4. Its construction pattern consists of: 1 front central room and 1 rear central room, 2 wings and 4 corridors. The rooms and corridors are connected with each other. It is a traditional residence of an aristocratic family.
   建筑格局为前后堂、两厢四廊，楼轩相接，廊庑回环，属传统的世家府第住宅。

Task 2

Passage Reading

isten to the short passage for the first time. Then practise it by reading it aloud by yourself.

City Sightseeing and Transportation Item 5

Xikou of Fenghua

Xikou of Fenghua, the home town of Chiang Kai-shek, covers an area of 379.6 square kilometers and has a population of nearly 100,000. It is divided into 114 administrative villages. Now it has become a scenic site of four-A state-level scenic resort. **Its human culture and natural scene are famous both at home and abroad.** There are a lot of famous scenic spots, such as Fenghao House (the Former Residence of Chiang Kai-shek), Wenchang Pavilion (the Former Residence of Song Meiling), Yutai Salt Shop (the birth place of Chiang Kai-shek), the Former Residence of Jiang Jingguo, the Xuedou Temple, the Qianzhangyan Waterfall, the Miaogao Terrace, the Sanyin Lake, and so on.

Fenghao House is Chiang's former residence, also one of the key scenic spots in the state-level Xikou scenic Site. **It is located at the lower street of Wuling Road in Xikou.** It faces south and looks over the street. It is named "Fenghao" and its other name is "Suju". **In front of the house is Shan Stream which is flowing by all the year.** The house is also quite opposite the famous Bijia Hill. The house covers an area of 4800 square meters including a floor space of 1850 square meters. There are 49 big and small rooms in it. **Its construction pattern consists of: 1 front central room and 1 rear central room, 2 wings and 4 corridors. The rooms and corridors are connected with each other. It is a traditional residence of an aristocratic family.** From the history, structure, decoration and application of Fenghao House, you can find out a lot of ways of Chiang's world and temperament of their life. It would be a great pleasure for a variety of visitors to see Chiang's former residence with their own eyes.

Task 3

Listen and Answer

You will hear five questions. Listen carefully and give an appropriate answer to each of them.

(1) _____
(2) _____
(3) _____
(4) _____
(5) _____

Task 4

Oral Practice

Retell the text in your own words.

Task 5

More Oral and Listening Practice:
【Listening】 Listen to the dialog & passage and fill in the blanks.

Listening I

On the Plane

A: Ladies and gentlemen, now we're on the plane to New York, first you should find your seats and place your luggage in order. If you have any questions, you can ask me.

B: Hello, _____?

A: Of course. 20A._____. It's a window seat.

B: Thank you. By the way, where can I put my bag?

A: _____.

B: Like this?

A: Yes, that's fine.

B: What are all these buttons and plugs in the arm rest?

A: Well, this one is the seat-recliner button. If you push the button, _____ But for take-off and landing, the seat must be in an upright position.

B: And this one?

A: Wait. Don't push that. That's call button. If you need the stewardess for anything, _____ and she'll come to see what you need.

B: Oh, I see.

A: Sir, please don't smoke until we are airborne and the "No Smoking" sign is turned off.

B: Oh, sorry.

A: _____ and your seat is in the upright position.

B: OK. Thank you.

City Sightseeing and Transportation   Item 5

Listening II

Ningbo

As an old cultural city with a clear _____ of four seasons and _____ climate, Ningbo has nurtured many talented people. There are 225 _____ relics in Ningbo, among which the Hemudu Cultural Relics has a history of 7000 years. The Tianyi Building is the oldest _____ building in China. The Baoguo temple is the oldest _____ one on the upper reaches of the Yangtze river. The Yue Kiln in Shanglin is one of the origins of Chinese _____. The ancient irrigation works in Tashanyan together with the former residence of Chiang Kaishek are both important cultural relics under national _____. Besides, the Tiantong temple is the No. 2 temple to advocate Zen Sect. The Ayuwang Temple has in it the mummy of Sakyamuni. The Xuedou Temple is a _____ rite of Maitreya and a resort where people pay respect to Buddhism. The Dongqian Lake is the biggest _____ lake in Zhejiang province. These _____, together with Putuo Mountains on its east, Yandang Mountains on its south, West Lake on its west and Shanghai on its east, are sure to make Ningbo a nice place for _____ from all over the world.

【Topics】 Divide the class into groups. Choose one of the following topics to discuss in each group. Give a short report about the group's opinion after that.

1. Most airlines now sell electronic tickets. What are their advantages and disadvantage?
2. What kind of life do you prefer, a busy life in big cities or a leisurely and simple life in the country? Why?
3. Comment on the statement "Eating is the utmost important part of life" by Confucius.

Item 6 The Service of Travel Destinations

旅游目的地服务

Model 1:
   Narrations on Tour   沿途讲解

Model 2:
   At the Ticket Box   在售票处

Model 3:
   Asking the Way   问路

Model 4:
   The Role of a Tour Guide   导游的职责

The Service of Travel Destinations   Item 6

Model 1
Narrations on Tour　沿途讲解

Task 1

Warm-up

Work in pairs. Try to talk about the question with your partner. " On the way to the scenic spots, as a guide, what should you tell your tourists before arriving? ".

Task 2

Learning Points

Listen to the following *words* and *useful expressions* and repeat. Then try to memorize them.

Words and Phrases

dedicate	['dedikeit]	v.	献出
schedule	['skedʒjul]	n.	时间表，一览表，计划
enlist	[in'list]	v.	参与，支持
UNESCO	[juːˈneskəu]	n.	联合国教育科学文化组织
resemble	[ri'zembl]	v.	相似，类似，像
serrate	['serit]	adj.	锯齿状的
zigzag	['zigzæg]	v.	使成锯齿形，蜿蜒
undulate	['ʌndjuleit]	adj.	波动的，起伏的
visible	['vizəbl]	adj.	可见的，看得见的
fortification	[ˌfɔːtifi'keiʃən]	n.	防御工事，尤指堡垒、要塞城墙等
defense	[di'fens]	n.	防卫，防卫物
invasion	[in'veiʒən]	n.	侵入，入侵
dynasty	['dinəsti]	n.	朝代，王朝
miracle	['mirəkl]	n.	奇迹
belong	[bi'lɔŋ]	v.	属于
fit as a fiddle			精神良好，状态良好
head for			取向于

| Peking Opera | 京剧 |
| The World Heritage | 世界遗产 |

Useful Expressions

1. Can all of you hear me?
   大家都能听到我说的话吗?
2. Now we're heading for it.
   我们现在就到那儿去。
3. The tour will start at 8 o'clock and will last four hours.
   这次旅游将在8点开始,并持续四小时。
4. And then in the evening we'll have a chance to enjoy a tea stop at the Laoshe Teahouse and a Peking Opera is also in our schedule.
   然后在晚上我们将有机会在老舍茶馆品茶并且欣赏京剧。
5. The Great Wall was enlisted in the World Heritage by UNESCO in 1987.
   1987年,长城被联合国教科文组织列为世界遗产。
6. Before you go, please take care of your personal belongings.
   在你们出发之前,请保管好你们的私人物品。

Task 3

Dialogue I

Listen to the *dialogue I* for the first time. Then practise the dialogue by reading it aloud with your partner. Read through it at least twice, changing your role each time.

Narrations on Tour

G: guide   T: tourist(s)

G: Good morning, everyone! **Can all of you hear me?**
T: Yes, very clearly.
G: How are you doing today?
T: We are fit as a fiddle! Thank you!
G: So are you ready for touring?
T: Yes, of course.
G: Let's get to business. First of all, let me tell you the itinerary today. We'll start today's trip with a visit to the Great Wall. **Now we're heading for it.**
T: How long will the bus trip take to get there?
G: About half an hour. **The tour will start at 8 o'clock and will last four hours.** Then we'll have a lunch nearby. This afternoon is dedicated to the Beijing Hutong. **And then in the evening we'll have**

The Service of Travel Destinations Item 6

a chance to enjoy a tea stop at the Laoshe Teahouse and a Peking Opera is also in our schedule. I hope all of you have a wonderful trip today. Now I'd like to tell about Great Wall. **The Great Wall was enlisted in the World Heritage by UNESCO in 1987.** It resembles a huge, serrated wall zigzagging its way to the east and west along the undulating mountains. It is said to be visible from the moon. Sections of earlier fortifications were connected to form a united defense system against invasions from the north throughout centuries.

T: When did it take on its present form?
G: During the Ming Dynasty from 1368 to 1644.
T: It must be a great miracle!
G: Absolutely!
   (*Half an hour later.*)
G: OK, here we are. It's time to get off the bus. **Before you go, please take care of your personal belongings.**
   (*They arrive at the entrance to the Great Wall.*)
G: Attention, please! Now, we're going to visit the Great Wall, please do remember that we will assemble right at the main gate at 12:30. Thank you.
T: What's the number of the bus?
G: It's 288120. Have a nice trip!

Task 4

Listen and Answer

You will hear five questions. Listen carefully and give an appropriate answer to each of them.

(1) _____
(2) _____
(3) _____
(4) _____
(5) _____

Task 5

Role-play

Act out the following dialogs.

【Situation A】 The local guide is taking a group of tourists to visit the Great Wall, now they are heading for it.

Local guide:
- ☆ Greets everyone.
- ☆ Asks whether they are ready for touring.
- ☆ Introduces the itinerary.
- ☆ Tells that the bus trip will take one hour.
- ☆ Gives a brief introduction of the Great Wall.
- ☆ Answers the tourists' questions.
- ☆ (When they arrive at the gate of Great Wall), tells the tourists to take care of personal belongings and when and where they will assemble, and the number of bus.
- ☆ Wishes to have a nice trip.

Tourists:
- ☆ Greet the local guide.
- ☆ Express the anxiety of touring.
- ☆ Ask that how long the bus trip takes to get Great Wall.
- ☆ Ask some questions about the Great Wall, such as: its building time, its stories and so on.
- ☆ Express thanks.

【**Situation B**】 Xiao Lu, a tour guide, is taking a group of tourists to visit Mogao Grottos, on the way to it, tourists ask some questions about the Mogao Grottos and Xiao Lu answers these questions.

Model 2
At the Ticket Box 在售票处

Task 1

Warm-up

Work in pairs. Try to translate the following words into Chinese and answer the question below.

| Cultural tourism | Religious tourism | Historical tourism | Leisure travel |
| Urban tourism | Eco-tourism | Business tourism | |

Which type of travel activities do you like best? Why?

Task 2

Learning Points

Listen to the following *words* and *useful expressions* and repeat. Then try to memorize them.

The Service of Travel Destinations   Item 6

Words and Phrases

admission	[əd'miʃən]	n.	许可，承认
schedule	['skedʒjul]	n.	行程表
memorial	[mi'mɔ:riəl]	adj.	记忆的
the all-in-one package			套价
Shen Garden			沈园
Orchid Pavilion			兰亭
Temple and Tomb of Yu The Great			大禹陵
East Lake			东湖
Three-Flavour Study			三味书屋

Useful Expressions

1. We offer the all-in-one package.
   我们提供套票。
2. What can I expect to see at these places?
   在这些地方我能看到什么？
3. They are free.
   它们是免费的。
4. RMB 20 Yuan for each.
   每张售价20元。
5. Here are the tickets.
   给您票。

Task 3

Dialogue II

Listen to the *dialogue II* for the first time. Then practise the dialogue by reading it aloud with your partner. Read through it at least twice, changing your role each time.

At the Ticket Box

【Scene】 *At the ticket box, the ticket clerk is answering the enquiries of a tourist.*

S: staff   T: tourist

S: Welcome to the hometown of Lu Xun, Shaoxing.
T: I'd like two admission tickets, please.
S: OK. **We offer the all-in-one package.**
T: What does the package include?

S: You pay once for all the four scenic spots and services.
T: **What can I expect to see at these places?**
S: You may visit the Lu Xun Memorial Hall, Lu Xun Former Residence, Three-Flavour Study and Hundred-Plant Garden.
T: Sounds interesting. What about other sights? Do I need to pay extra for them?
S: Yes, I'm afraid so. You also can enjoy the beautiful scenes in Shen Garden, Orchid Pavilion, Temple and Tomb of Yu The great and East Lake.
T: I see. Can you give me a program schedule and a map?
S: Here you are. **They are free.**
T: How much is each ticket?
S: **RMB 20 Yuan for each.** Did you say you need two?
T: Yes, here is the money.
S: Thank you, sir. **Here are the tickets.** Have a nice day.

Task 4

Listen and Answer

You will hear five questions. Listen carefully and give an appropriate answer to each of them.

(1) _____
(2) _____
(3) _____
(4) _____
(5) _____

Task 5

Role-play

Act out the following dialogs.

【Situation A】 A couple arrive at the ticket box located at the main entrance to the Putuo Mountain.

Staff:
☆ Greets the couple.
☆ Introduces the scenic spots.
☆ Offers the price of each ticket.
☆ Recommends restaurants.
☆ Shows the location of a bank nearby.

The Service of Travel Destinations   Item 6

Tourist:
- ☆ Wishes to buy two tickets.
- ☆ Asks what they can see.
- ☆ Wants to know price of ticket.
- ☆ Asks about where to dine.
- ☆ Wants to know where to draw money from their bank account.

【Situation B】You are a guide and take a group of tourisms to visit Palace Museum. At the ticket box, you should buy tickets for them.

Model 3
Asking the Way   问路

Task 1

Warm-up

Work in pairs. You have just arrived at a city's railway station. Please tell your partner how to get to the hotel.

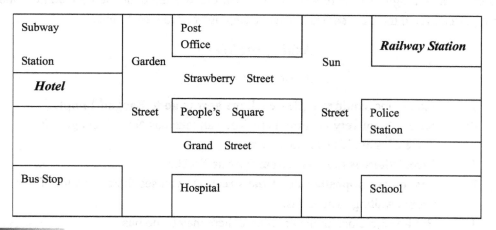

Task 2

Learning Points

Listen to the following *words* and *useful expressions* and repeat. Then try to memorize them.

Words and Phrases

stop	[stɔp]	n.	车站
sign	[sain]	n.	标记
opposite side			对面
subway station			地铁
peak time			高峰期

Useful Expressions

1. Could you please tell me how to go to Baoguo Temple?
   你可以告诉我保国寺怎么去吗?
2. Where is the bus station for bus No.10?
   10路车的车站在什么地方?
3. Just on the opposite side of the street.
   就在街对面。
4. Keep going straight along the road until you see the big blue subway sign.
   沿着这条街笔直下去直到你看到那个大大的蓝色地铁标志。

Task 3

Dialogue III

Listen to the *dialogue III* for the first time. Then practise the dialogue by reading it aloud with your partner. Read through it at least twice, changing your role each time.

Asking the Way

T: tourist   P: passerby

T: Excuse me, **could you please tell me how to go to Baoguo Temple?**

P: Sure. It's not very far from here. You can take bus No. 10 and get off at the 2nd stop, it's two stops away.

T: I see. **Where is the bus station for bus No.10?**

P: **Just on the opposite side of the street.** Do you see there are a lot of people waiting? There it is.

T: But it is 5 o'clock in the afternoon, there may be no bus.

P: Yes, you're right. So you can take the subway.

T: By the way, where's the subway station?

P: The subway station is a little further on. Cross the street and turn around, and take the first turning on the right. **Keep going straight along the road until you see the big blue** subway sign. There it is

The Service of Travel Destinations   Item 6

T: How long dose it take me to get there?
P: Oh, you can walk it within 20 minutes.
T: That' fine. Then I would rather take the subway at such a peak time. Thank you so much.
P: You're welcome.

Task 4

Listen and Answer

You will hear five questions. Listen carefully and give an appropriate answer to each of them.

(1) _____
(2) _____
(3) _____
(4) _____
(5) _____

Task 5

Role-play

Act out the following dialogs.

【Situation A】 Work in a group of two or three, and use the following map as a guide and make up conversations asking the way and giving directions.

Summer Palace	Beijing University	Zhongguancun Street	Tsinghua University
			Beijing Modern Plaza
Third Ring North Road			To Airport
Beijing Friendship Hotel		Zhongguancun South Street	Shuang'an Market
			Capital Gym Beijing Zoo
Beijing Institute of Technology Central University for Nationalities			To Tian'anmen

Model 4
The Role of a Tour Guide　导游的职责

Task 1

Learning Points

Listen to the following *words* and *useful expressions* and repeat. Then try to memorize them.

Words and Phrases

ensure	[inˈʃuə]	v.	确保，保证
maximum	[ˈmæksiməm]	adj.	最多的，最大极限
satisfaction	[ˌsætisˈfækʃən]	n.	满意
particular	[pəˈtikjulə]	adj.	独特的，特别的，挑剔的
supervise	[ˈsju:pəvaiz]	v.	监督，管理，指导
complaint	[kəmˈpleint]	n.	抱怨
coordinate	[kəuˈɔ:dinit]	v.	协调，整合
co-operation	[co-ˌɔpəˈreiʃən]	n.	合作，协作
supplement	[ˈsʌplimənt]	n.	补充
accurate	[ˈækjurit]	adj.	准确的，精确的

Useful Expressions

1. The tour guide should do everything possible to ensure that tour members obtain the maximum enjoyment and satisfaction from the tour.
   导游应该竭尽所能确保每一个游客在旅游中获得最大限度的享受和满足。
2. The tour guide should pay particular attention to the health and safety of the tour members.
   导游应该尤其关注游客的健康和安全。
3. Do everything possible to become knowledgeable about the cities and sites included in the itinerary of each trip he/she leads.
   导游应该竭尽所能对每一次行程所涉及的城市和景点有足够的了解。

The Service of Travel Destinations   Item 6

Task 2

Learning Points

Listen to the short passage for the first time. Then practise it by reading it aloud by yourself.

The Role of a Tour Guide

(1) **The tour guide should do everything possible to ensure that tour members obtain the maximum enjoyment and satisfaction from the tour.**
(2) **The tour guide should pay particular attention to the health and safety of the tour members.**
(3) The tour guide should supervise the transporting of the tour members' luggage.
(4) Assist the tour members in their dealings with airlines, hotels and other principals. For example, if a tour member's luggage is lost or damaged, help the tour member file a complaint with airline or the department connected.
(5) Coordinate all arrangements in co-operation with the hotels and local tour guide(s). If a tour needs a single room on his/her own, the tour guide should check the hotel first and pays a single supplement on the spot.
(6) **Do everything possible to become knowledgeable about the cities and sites included in the itinerary of each trip he/she leads.**
(7) File complete and accurate trip reports.

Task 3

Listen and Answer

You will hear five questions. Listen carefully and give an appropriate answer to each of them.

(1) _____
(2) _____
(3) _____
(4) _____
(5) _____

Task 4

Oral Practice

Retell the text in your own words.

Task 5

More Oral and Listening Practice:

【Listening】 Listen to the dialog & passage and fill in the blanks.

Listening I

How to get to People's Square?

T: tourist   S: staff

T: Excuse me,_____?
S: By subway or by bus?
T: _____?
S: At this time of day,_____. It takes about
     10 to 20 minutes._____?
T: That would be most helpful. Thanks.
S: Sure, my pleasure. _____, right on the
     corner of Huaihai Road. You will see the signs with a red "H". Take
     _____the People's Square Station.
T: _____. Thank you.
S: You're welcome. Hope you will enjoy your day.

Listening II

The Global Concept of Tour Guide Service

The global _____ of tour guide service _____ 7 meanings represented by the word "SERVICE" with 7 letters.

S: it is "smile, the tour guide should _____ smiling service.
E: excellent. Service should be _____ in an excellent way.
R: ready. The tour guide is constantly _____ to serve tourists.
V: viewing. Each tourist should be _____ as a _____ guest
     requiring his or her _____ care.
I: inviting. Tourists will be invited to _____ after he/she leaves the city
     or the country.
C: creating. The tour guide should create an amiable and _____
     environment for tourists.
E: eye. Each tour guide pays a close _____to tourists with
     keen _____, anticipates their needs and provides his or her

service in time which makes tourists feel that they are _____ and constantly _____ by the tour guide.

【Topics】 Divide the class into groups. Choose one of the following topics to discuss in each group. Give a short report about the group's opinion after that.

1. Why should a foreign traveler have proper reasons to apply for visa extension?
2. Can you describe your experience of showing a classmate or relative around your hometown? What problems did you come across and how did you solve them?
3. What influences have the philosophies of Confucianism, Taoism, yin and yang exerted on the development of Chinese culinary arts respectively?

Item 7 Tour of Gardens

园 林 游 览

Model 1:
　　A Trip to the Yu Yuan Garden　　游览豫园

Model 2:
　　Touring the Summer Palace　　游览颐和园

Model 3:
　　The Four Elements in a Traditional Garden
　　园林四要素

Model 4:
　　Suzhou Gardens　　苏州园林

Tour of Gardens   Item 7

Model 1
A Trip to the Yu Yuan Garden 游览豫园

Task 1

Warm-up

Work in pairs. This item we are going to take trips to different gardens in China. First let's carry out a brief discussion.

1. Discuss the standards by which Chinese gardens can be classified.

> ☆ Contents of gardens;
> ☆ Owners of gardens;
> ☆ Geographical location of gardens;

2. Can you translate the following gardens into Chinese and tell each other where they are located.

The Yuyuan Garden,	The Summer Palace,
The Chengde Mountain Summer Resort,	The Humble Administrator's Garden,
The Lingering Garden,	The Garden of Perfection and Brightness,
The Lion Grove Garden,	The Master-of-Nets Garden,
The Retreat and Reflection Garden,	The Grand View Garden.

3. Can you say something about the Yuyuan Garden? And what type of garden does the Yuyuan Garden belong to?

Task 2

Learning Points

Listen to the following *words* and *useful expressions* and repeat. Then try to memorize it.

Words and Phrases

backpacker   ['bæk,pækə]   n.   背包族，背包徒步旅行者

arched	[ɑːtʃt]	adj.	拱形的
ingenious	[inˈdʒiːnjəs]	adj.	精巧的，敏捷的
architecture	[ˈɑːkitektʃə]	n.	建筑
layout	[ˈleiˌaut]	n.	布局，设计
private	[ˈpraivit]	adj.	私人的
pavilion	[pəˈviljən]	n.	亭子
rockery	[ˈrɔkəri]	n.	假山，石园林
particularity	[pəˌtikjuˈlæriti]	n.	特别之处
peculiar	[piˈkjuːljə]	adj.	特殊的
announcement	[əˈnaunsmənt]	n.	宣告，通告
imperialist	[imˈpiəriəlist]	n.	帝国主义者
uprising	[ˈʌpˌraiziŋ]	n.	起义，暴动
patriotic	[ˌpætriˈɔtik, ˌpeitri-]	adj.	爱国主义的，爱国的
be characteristic of			具有……的特征
arched bridges			拱桥
twisting corridors and passages			回廊
the Hall for Summoning Spring			点春堂
the Small Sword Society			小刀会

Useful Expressions

1. Many tourists are attracted by its ingenious architecture and layout.
   许多游客被它独特的建筑风格和奇异的布局所吸引。
2. The buildings in the garden are characteristic of South China's style of the Ming and Qing dynasties.
   豫园的建筑具有江南明清的典型特征。
3. The rock looks somewhat different from the ordinary rocks.
   这块岩石看起来和普通石头有点不同。
4. The rock has four particularities.
   这块石头有四个特别之处。
5. It sounds instructive and patriotic.
   听起来具有教育意义和爱国情怀。

Task 3

Dialogue I

Listen to the *dialogue I* for the first time. Then practice the dialogue by reading them aloud with your partner. Read through it at least twice, changing your role each time.

Tour of Gardens Item 7

A Trip to the Yu Yuan Garden

【Scene】 *Miss Zhang, a guide from the Youth Travel Service; Jack, a foreign tourist. Miss Zhang is showing Jack around the Yuyuan Garden. Jack has a special interest in the ancient Chinese gardens.*

A: Miss Zhang   B: Jack

A: Jack, I know you are a backpacker. You may walk around the Yuyuan Garden yourself. Why do you want me to travel with you?

B: Well, you know, I'm from Canada. I want to know more about this garden. Besides, I don't want to take photos only.

A: The Yuyuan Garden is a very famous classical garden, a private garden of peace and comfort in meaning. Though the garden is not very large, **many tourists are attracted by its ingenious architecture and layout.**

B: A private garden! Who built it?

A: Pan Yunduan, a governor of Sichuan Province in the Ming Dynasty, built it to bring happiness and pleasure to his parents in their old age.

B: When was it constructed?

A: The building of the garden began in 1559 and was completed in 1577. It has a history of more than four centuries.

B: It's very attractive.

A: Yes. There are more than thirty different fascinating scenes in it. Look, pavilions, towers, rockeries and goldfish ponds are connected by arched bridges and twisting corridors and passages. **The buildings in the garden are characteristic of South China's style of the Ming and Qing dynasties.**

B: It's very special and graceful. I'm very interested.

A: Yes, you are right. Look, here is a special rock named Yu Linglong (the Exquisite Jade Rock). It is one of the most famous scenic spots in the Yuyuan Garden.

B: **The rock looks somewhat different from the ordinary rocks.**

A: Yes. **The rock has four particularities.**

B: What are they?

A: First, the rock has many holes in it. Second, its absorptive capacity is excellent. Third, it has good quality and finally its construction is peculiar.

B: How marvelous! I have never seen such a wonderful rock before. I'll take some pictures.

A: Jack, we're coming to the Hall for Summoning Spring, another important scene in the garden. It was once used as the headquarters of the Small Sword Society in 1853. The Small Sword Society was an uprising against the foreign imperialists in shanghai.

B: Well, **it sounds instructive and patriotic.**

Task 4

Listen and Answer

You will hear five questions. Listen carefully and give an appropriate answer to each of them.

(1) _____
(2) _____
(3) _____
(4) _____
(5) _____

Task 5

Role-play

Act out the following dialogs.

【Situation A】 Mr. Wang is a tour guide who is showing a team of tourists from Australia around the Yuyuan Garden.

Mr. Wang:
- ☆ Greets the tourists.
- ☆ Introduces the history of the Yuyuan Garden.
- ☆ Explains the ingenious architecture and layout.
- ☆ Explains Yu Linglong to tourists.
- ☆ Explains the Hall for Summoning Spring.

Tourists:
- ☆ Want to know the history of the Yuyuan Garden.
- ☆ Take pictures with the garden's gate as a background.
- ☆ Appreciate the fascinating scenes.
- ☆ Appreciate Yu Linglong.
- ☆ Give exciting remarks.

【Situation B】 Suppose you are a tour guide to accompany a group of tourists to visit the Chengde Mountain Summer Resort. Make up a simulated dialogue.

Tour of Gardens Item 7

Model 2
Touring the Summer Palace 游览颐和园

Task 1

Warm-up

Work in pairs and answer the questions below.

1. The Summer Palace is one of the most famous gardens in China. Have you been to the Summer Palace? Which attractions impress you most?
2. Can you say the Chinese names of the following English Proper names concerning the Summer Palace? Would you please introduce one or two scenic spots in English?

Anglo-French Allied forces, the Long Corridor,	the Western Dike, the Kunming Lake,
the Longevity Hill,	the Palace of Benevolent Longevity,
the Hall of Dispelling Clouds,	the Tower of Buddhist Incense,
the Garden of Harmonious Interest,	the Suzhou Shopping Street

Task 2

Learning Points

Listen to the following *words* and *useful expressions* and repeat. Then try to memorize it.

Words and Phrases

imperial	[im'piəriəl]	adj.	皇家的，皇帝的
bronze	[brɔnz]	n.	青铜
antler	['æntlə]	n.	鹿角
hoof	[hu:f]	n.	蹄子
hectare	['hekta:]	n.	公顷
corridor	['kɔridɔ:]	n.	走廊
extensive	[iks'tensiv]	adj.	广阔的，广泛的
summit	['sʌmit]	n.	顶峰，顶点
picturesque	[ˌpiktʃə'resk]	adj.	如画的，美丽的

the Longevity Hill 万寿山
Kunming Lake 昆明湖
the Long Corridor 长廊
the Palace of Benevolent Longevity 仁寿殿
the Hall of Dispelling Clouds 排云殿

Useful Expressions

1. We will put ourselves completely in your hands.
   我们完全听从你的安排。
2. Would you please take a photo of me here?
   请在这儿给我拍张照好吗?
3. It was believed that the animal could detect the disloyal persons, preventing them from entering.
   据说这种动物能够识别小人,不让他们入内。
4. The Summer Palace is the best-preserved and largest imperial garden in China.
   颐和园是中国保存最完整、最大的皇家园林。
5. I'm afraid one day is not enough to see all the interesting places.
   恐怕一天是看不完所有的景观。
6. We can have an extensive view of all the fascinating places.
   所有景色一览无余。
7. What fun it is for us to row boats on the lake!
   湖上放舟该多惬意呀!
8. After the short break, we will go to some other places worth visiting.
   短暂休息后,我们去别的值得一看的地方。

Task 3

Dialogue II

Listen to the *dialogue II* for the first time. Then practice the dialogue by reading them aloud with your partner. Read through it at least twice, changing your role each time.

Touring the Summer Palace

【Scene】 *Miss Liu, the tour guide, is leading a tour group into the Summer Palace for the visit.*

A: Miss Liu   B: tourists

A: Good morning, everyone. Today we are going to tour the Summer Palace, a very famous imperial garden in China.
B: All right. **We will put ourselves completely in your hands.**

Tour of Gardens   Item 7

A: Here we are. This is the Summer Palace.
B: Oh, the gate with one bronze lion on each side looks very magnificent. **Would you please take a photo of me here?**
A: Sure. Say "cheer"! OK. Please look at the bronze animal. This animal is peculiar because it has the head of a dragon, the antlers of a deer, the tail of a lion and the hooves of an ox.
B: So interesting. What functions does it have?
A: **It was believed that the animal could detect the disloyal persons, preventing them from entering.**
B: What a big garden! Can you tell us some information on it, Miss Liu?
A: Of course. **The Summer Palace is the best-preserved and largest imperial garden in China.** It covers an area of 290 hectares and has many palaces, pavilions, bridges and corridors in it.
B: Wonderful. **I'm afraid one day is not enough to see all the interesting places.** Where should we go first?
A: In the Summer Palace there are mainly three parts: palaces for political activities, religious buildings and living area. First let's climb the hill. This way please.
B: We're nearly on the top of the hill. Now, **we can have an extensive view of all the fascinating places.**
A: Wow, we succeed coming to the summit of the Longevity Hill. Look. That is the Kunming Lake. It is picturesque. The lake is man-made and covers three-fourths of this garden.
B: What a lovely view! **What fun it is for us to row boats on the lake!** Can we take a boat ride?
A: Of course, you can. Would you like to have a rest in that pavilion?
B: That's a good idea!
A: **After the short break, we will go to some other places worth visiting,** for example, the Long Corridor, the Palace of Benevolent Longevity, the Hall of Dispelling Clouds.
B: All right, we'll follow you.

Task 4

Listen and Answer

You will hear five questions. Listen carefully and give an appropriate answer to each of them.

(1) _____

(2) _____

(3) _____

(4) _____
(5) _____

Task 5

Role-play

Act out the following dialogs.

【Situation A】 Miss Deng is a tour guide who is leading a tour group of Canadian tourists in the Summer Palace. You are asked to act out a dialogue according to the following tips.

Miss Deng:
- ☆ Greets the tourists.
- ☆ Introduces today's itinerary.
- ☆ Interprets the lion at the gate of the Summer Palace.
- ☆ Explains the peculiar bronze animal to the tourists.
- ☆ Interprets the Longevity Hill.
- ☆ Explains Kunming Lake and other scenic attractions.

Tourists:
- ☆ Greet the tour guide, Miss Deng.
- ☆ Ask to take a picture.
- ☆ Ask the tour guide for some basic information about the Summer Palace.
- ☆ Give exciting remarks on the top of the Longevity Hill.
- ☆ Suggest rowing boats on Kunming Lake.
- ☆ Visit other scenic attractions.

【Situation B】 Suppose you are an English tour guide and will usher your American friend George to visit the Forbidden City.

Tour guide:
- ☆ This is the world-famous Forbidden City where emperors and their families lived.
- ☆ 24 emperors of the Ming and Qing Dynasties. It was first built in 1406, the Ming Dynasty.
- ☆ It is the largest and best-preserved palace complex in China and one of the most magnificent ancient palace complexes in the world. The entire building complex can be divided into two parts: the inner palaces and the outer palaces.
- ☆ They have different functions. The inner palaces were the emperors' residential area while the outer palaces were places to handle state affairs.
- ☆ It's called the Hall of Supreme Harmony, which is the most spectacular of all the palace buildings and also the largest hall built entirely of wood in China. It's one of the three

Tour of Gardens　　Item 7

halls of the outer palaces that are the Hall of Supreme Harmony（太和殿）, the Hall of Complete Harmony（中和殿）and the Hall of Preserving Harmony（保和殿）.
☆ It was the most important place for emperors to handle all official business. Ceremonies such as grand celebration, emperor's birthday all took place here.
☆ Yes. The throne symbolized the supreme power of the feudal emperors.

George:
☆ How many emperors once lived here?
☆ Wow, 24 emperors! Though it has a history of over 500 years, it still looks elaborate and picturesque.
☆ What are differences between them?
☆ I see. What's the grand hall?
☆ What's the use of the Hall of Supreme Harmony?
☆ Is that the emperor's throne on top of the platform?

【**Situation C**】 You are a guide and your are required to make up a dialogue to introduce the Long Corridor in the Summer Palace to the tourists

Model 3
The Four Elements in a Traditional Garden　　园林四要素

Task 1

Warm-up

Work in pairs. Suppose you are a guide, and you are going to introduce major elements of a classical garden and their functions to your guests, what will you say to them? Discuss with your partner.

Task 2

Learning Points

Listen to the following *words* and *useful expressions* and repeat. Then try to memorize them.

Words and Phrases

imitation　　　　　[imi'teiʃən]　　　　　　　　n.　　　　　　　仿制品

microcosm	['maikrəkɔz(ə)m]	n.	微观世界
landscape	['lændskeip]	n.	风景，景色
architecture	['ɑːkitektʃə]	n.	建筑
artificial	[aːtiˈfiʃəl]	adj.	人造的，人工的
fountain	['fauntin]	n.	喷泉
insight	['insait]	n.	洞察力，见识
lively	['laivli]	adj.	生气勃勃的
symbolize	['simbəlaiz]	vt.	象征
longevity	[lɔnˈdʒeviti]	n.	长寿，长命
perseverance	[ˌpəːsiˈviərəns]	n.	坚持不懈
endurance	[inˈdjurəns]	n.	忍耐力
clean-handedness		n.	清廉
lotus	['ləutəs]	n.	荷花，莲花
harmonious	[hɑːˈməunjəs]	adj.	和谐的
man of letters			文人，学者
outstanding feature			突出特点

Useful Expressions

1. I have got the impression that many Chinese gardens have the similar pattern.
   我有这样的印象，许多中国园林模式相似。

2. A Classical garden should include the four basic elements: mountains, waters, plants and architecture.
   传统园林的四要素包括山石，水体，植物和建筑。

3. The rockery built of individual stones is one of the most outstanding features of the Chinese garden.
   由石头堆成的假山是中国园林最突出的特点之一。

4. Water was the central element for it provides movement, coolness and sounds within the garden.
   水是园林的关键因素，能给园林带来动感、凉爽和水声。

5. I'm beginning to get an insight into your "mountain and water culture".
   我开始了解你们的山水文化。

6. Pine trees, for instance, symbolized longevity, perseverance and bitter endurance.
   譬如，松树象征着长寿、坚持不懈和坚贞不屈。

Task 3

Dialogue III

Listen to the *dialogue III* for the first time. Then practise the dialogue by reading it aloud

Tour of Gardens Item 7

with your partner. Read through it at least twice, changing your role each time.

The Four Elements in a Traditional Garden

【Scene】 *Miss Wang, a tour guide, is trying to explain the four basic elements of a classical garden to the foreign tourists.*

A: Miss Wang   B: tourists from Canada.

B: Miss Wang, **I have got the impression that many Chinese gardens have the similar pattern.** Why is that?

A: Well, people have been following a basic principle in building a garden, which is an imitation of Nature or as many people like to call it, a "microcosm of Nature".

B: You mean the landscape?

A: Not only the landscape. **A Classical garden should include the four basic elements: mountains, waters, plants and architecture.**

B: I see. But what if there is a limitation on size for a garden?

A: Then artificial hills would be piled up instead of a natural mountain. **The rockery built of individual stones is one of the most outstanding features of the Chinese garden.**

B: What about the waters?

A: The water areas, either natural or man-made, include lakes, rivers, ponds, streams, waterfalls and fountains. **Water is the central element for it provides movement, coolness and sounds within the garden.** In garden designing mountains and waters usually go together.

B: Yeah, **I'm beginning to get an insight into your "mountain and water culture".**

A: Very good. Let's go on to plants, the liveliest part of a garden.

B: That is easy to understand. They can add much natural beauty to a garden.

A: Right, but more than that. The trees and flowers were carefully chosen to show the owner's special personality and preference.

B: I have no idea about that.

A: **Pine trees, for instance, symbolized longevity, perseverance and bitter endurance.** And lotus, one of the favorite flowers of man of letters in the past, represented purity, clean-handedness.

B: Thanks, Miss Wang. What about the last element, architecture?

A: Architecture is the most human part of a garden. It appears in different styles, such as a pavilion, a temple, a corridor, a tower, a bridge and a palace, to create the harmonious man-made beauty in a garden.

B: Thanks a lot. I have a better understanding of a Chinese garden.

Task 4

Listen and Answer

You will hear five questions. Listen carefully and give an appropriate answer to each of them.

(1) _____
(2) _____
(3) _____
(4) _____
(5) _____

Task 5

Role-play

Act out the following dialogs.

【Situation A】 Miss Wang, a tour guide, continues to explain the four basic elements of a classical garden to the foreign tourists.

Tourists:
- ☆ Ask for the trees typically chosen in a traditional Chinese garden.
- ☆ Ask for the flowers usually planted in a garden.
- ☆ Ask for the animals often raised in a traditional garden.
- ☆ Wonder the reasons for raising animals in a garden.
- ☆ Want to know how architecture can be human because Miss Wang says "Architecture is the most human part of a garden".
- ☆ Ask for the meaning of "frustrations".
- ☆ Express thanks.

Miss Wang:
- ☆ Introduces typical trees including pine trees, bamboos, maples, and plum trees.
- ☆ Introduces the usual flowers: lotus flowers, peach flowers, orchid, plum flowers, osmanthus flowers.
- ☆ Answers the typical animals including deer, cranes, swans, peacocks, and goldfish.
- ☆ Explains the reasons with examples: male and female cranes are loyal to each other until their old age; the goldfish symbolizes property and wealth.
- ☆ Tells the concrete reasons: the architectural buildings can reveal the level of building techniques and kinds of materials used in different periods. And the literary decorations on the buildings such as paintings, calligraphy, couplets, poems and furniture all

Tour of Gardens   Item 7

expressed the owner's special experiences and frustrations.
☆ Tells that many owners were retired or dismissed officials or men of letters who had never had any chances and they were seeking quiet places to escape from the "busy world", or in modern term "go back to Nature".

【Situation B】You are asked to discuss and make a dialogue on the representative significance of pine trees, bamboos and plums respectively in the Chinese traditional culture.

Model 4
Suzhou Gardens 苏州园林

Task 1

Learning Points

Listen to the following *words* and *useful expressions* and repeat. Then try to memorize them.

Words and Phrases

paradise	['pærədaiz]	n.	天堂
wonderland	['wʌndəlænd]	n.	仙境，奇异的地方
tranquil	['træŋkwil]	adj.	宁静的，平静的
exquisite	['ekskwizit]	adj.	高雅的，精巧的
in good condition			保存良好的
Venice in the East			东方威尼斯
the Humble Administrator's Garden			拙政园
the Lion Grove Garden			狮子林
the Lingering Garden			留园
the Master-of-Nets Garden			网师园
the Lotus Garden			藕园
the Pavilion of the Surging Waves			沧浪亭
the Chengde Mountain Summer Resort			承德避暑山庄
the World Heritage List			世界遗产名录
Kingdom of Rockeries			假山王国

Useful Expressions

1. Suzhou is one of the oldest cultural cities in China, a place of great beauty, and a

wonderland of rivers and gardens.
苏州是我国最古老的文化名城之一，风景非常优美，河流交错，园林密布。

2. The gardens south of the Yangtze River are the best under Heaven, and among them the gardens of Suzhou are the best.
江南园林甲天下，苏州园林甲江南。

3. Suzhou is unique in terms of the number of gardens, their tranquil environment, refined layout and exquisite building style.
苏州的独特之处在于园林的数量，静谧的环境，精巧的布局和高雅的建筑风格。

4. The Pavilion of the Surging Waves is known for its tranquil scenery and simple architecture.
沧浪亭以它宁静的环境和简约的建筑风格而闻名。

5. Suzhou deserves the fame of a human paradise on earth.
苏州不愧为人间天堂啊。

Task 2

Passage Reading

Listen to the short passage for the first time. Then practice it by reading it aloud by yourself.

Suzhou Gardens

Suzhou is one of the oldest cultural cities in China, a place of great beauty, and a wonderland of rivers and gardens. It has always renowned as a "paradise on earth" and the "Venice in the East". One well-known proverb says "Paradise in heaven, Suzhou and Hangzhou on earth". Another old saying goes, **"The gardens south of the Yangtze River are the best under Heaven, and among them the gardens of Suzhou are the best."**

Suzhou is unique in terms of the number of gardens, their tranquil environment, refined layout and exquisite building style. The masterpieces of classical gardens, still in good condition, include the Humble Administrator's Garden, the Lion Grove Garden, the Lingering Garden, the Master-of-Nets Garden, the Lotus Garden and the Pavilion of the Surging Waves. The unique charm of these gardens led to their entry into the World Heritage List in 1997 and 2000.

The Humble Administrator's Garden is one of the four classical gardens in China, together with the Summer Palace in Beijing, the Chengde Mountain Summer Resort, and Lingering Garden in Suzhou. It's also the largest of the four famous classical gardens in Suzhou, the other three being the Pavilion of the Surging Waves, the Lion Grove Garden and the Lingering Garden.

The Pavilion of the Surging Waves is known for its tranquil scenery

Tour of Gardens   Item 7

and simple architecture. The garden has long corridors along the banks of the ponds. The Lion Grove Garden, renowned as a "Kingdom of Rockeries", is exquisite and imaginative in its design of rockeries. Stones in the garden take on different interesting shapes of lions, lying, sitting and standing. The Lingering Garden consists of four sections: rockeries in the west, picturesque scenery in the north, hall and pavilion structures in the east, and hills and waters at the center. A winding corridor of over 700 meters links them.

Suzhou deserves the fame of a human paradise on earth.

Task 3

Listen and Answer

You will hear five questions. Listen carefully and give an appropriate answer to each of them.

(1) _____
(2) _____
(3) _____
(4) _____
(5) _____

Task 4

Oral Practice

Retell the text in your own words.

Task 5

More Oral and Listening Practice:
【Listening】 *Listen to the dialogs and fill in the blanks.*

Listening I

Touring the Grand View Garden

A: Today we are going to visit the famous Grand View Garden. Our bus will stop at a small bridge and we'll climb the nearby tower to _____ _____ the Grand View Garden. _____. Look at these buildings with white wall and black roofs.

B: _____!
A: Yes, it is a typical garden in the south of the Yangtze River. Now we'd like to see a screen wall.
B: _____?
A: Yes, but we have to go around the screen wall.
B: Aha, why does the screen wall stand in the way?
A: _____. And it also makes it more difficult for evil spirits to enter.
B: _____.
A: _____?
B: No. I've never been to these places in China before.
A: Now we will walk through the heavy red gate and into the courtyards with unique styles. Just ahead, there is a group of strange rocks, ponds and willows. Among them is the home of Jia Baoyu, one major character of *The Story of Stones* by Cao Xueqin.
B: _____!

Listening II

Visiting the Chengde Mountain Summer Resort

A: It is said that the Chengde Mountain Summer Resort is the largest surviving imperial garden complex in China. _____ Is that true?

B: Yes, it covers a area of 5.6 million square meters which is twice the size of the Summer Palace. And the mountain resort consists of a palace area and a scenery area. _____?

A: _____ since we have visited many palaces in Beijing. The palaces here are mostly made from dark hardwood. In the scenery area, there is a big lake. Lotuses and pines grow around.

B: Ok. Let's go around the scenery area first. Look, _____, reminding one of the land South of the Yangtze River. And the water in the lake is so clear and blue.

A: The hill over there is called the Gold Hill. _____. Standing on the top of the hill, _____. Is there a spring flowing out of the cracks in the north of the Gold Hill?

B: Yes. It is called the Warm River Spring.

A: Oh, look at the peak on the east.

B: It looks like an inverted washing club, so people call it the Club Peak （棒槌峰）. It's so unique.

Tour of Gardens　　Item 7

A: _____. This kind of beautiful scenery is rare in the north of China. I feel as if I were in a different world.

B: _____?

A: That's a good idea.

【Topics】 Divide the class into groups. Choose one of the following topics to discuss in each group. Give a short report about the group's opinion after that.

1. Give a brief oral introduction to classical gardens in China such as their types, features, locations and their representative masterpieces.
2. Discuss and make a guide commentary concerning a famous garden in China.
3. What differences do you know about the table manners in China and in the Western countries?

Item 8 Tour of Mountains

山、水之旅

Model 1:
　　On Huangshan　　黄山之旅

Model 2:
　　A Trip in Guilin　　游览桂林

Model 3:
　　Huangguoshu Waterfalls　　黄果树瀑布

Model 4:
　　West Lake　　西湖

Tour of Mountains   Item 8

Model 1
On Huangshan   黄山之旅

Task 1

Warm-up

Work in pairs. Discuss the following questions with your partner.

1. Have you been to Mount Huangshan? Which scenic spots impress you most deeply?
2. Could you name the three main peaks and the four wonders of Mount Huangshan in English?

Task 2

Learning Points

Listen to the following *words* and *useful expressions* and repeat. Then try to memorize them.

Words and Phrases

odd	[ɔd]	*adj.*	奇怪的
grotesque	[grəuˈtesk]	*adj.*	奇形怪状的
world-renowned		*adj.*	世界闻名的
curative	[ˈkjuərətiv]	*adj.*	能治病的
marvelous	[ˈmaːviləs]	*adj.*	奇妙的，了不起的
odd pines			奇松
grotesque rocks			怪石
cloud seas			云海
hot springs			温泉
the Guest-Greeting Pine			迎客松
the See-the-Guest-off Pine			送客松
the Phoenix Pine			凤凰松
the Black Tiger Pine			黑虎松
the Flower of a Dreaming Pen			梦笔生花

Monkey Gazing at the sea	猴子观海
the Turtle Peak	鳌鱼峰
the Five Sacred Mountains	五岳

Useful Expressions

1. Wow, what beautiful scenery! Can we get off the coach and take some pictures?
   哇，多美的风景！我们下车拍些照片吧。
2. Look ahead! Have you seen pine trees on that peak with such shapely leaves?
   朝前看！你们看见山顶那些形态优美的黄山松吗？
3. Mount Huangshan is world-renowned for its four wonders.
   黄山因四绝而闻名于世。
4. The Guest-Greeting Pine always stretches out its arms to welcome guests all over the world.
   迎客松总是伸出双臂欢迎五湖四海的宾客。
5. The mountain's grotesque rocks are given fancy names such as the Flower of a Dreaming Pen, Monkey Gazing at the sea, and Turtle Peak.
   黄山怪石冠以奇特的名称，如梦笔生花，猴子观海，鳌鱼峰。
6. Mount Huangshan deserves the fame for "No. 1 Mountain under Heaven"!
   黄山不愧为"天下第一山"的美称。
7. One visits no mountains after the Five Sacred Mountains. And after Mount Huangshan, one has no eye for the Five Sacred Mountains.
   五岳归来不看山，黄山归来不看岳。

Task 3

Dialogue I

Listen to the *dialogue I* for the first time. Then practise the dialogue by reading it aloud with your partner. Read through it at least twice, changing your role each time.

On Huangshan

A: *Miss Qin, a local tour guide*   B: *tourists from the Great Britain*

A: Ladies and gentlemen, attention, please. We are reaching the foot of Mount Huangshan.
B: **Wow, what beautiful scenery! Can we get off the coach and take some pictures?**
A: Sure. Now the coach has stopped. Please get off the coach one by one. **Look ahead! Have you seen pine trees on that peak with such**

Tour of Mountains Item 8

shapely leaves?
B: Yes, terrific! They have odd shapes.
A: As mentioned on the bus, Mount Huangshan is called "No. 1 Mountain under Heaven". **It is world-renowned for its four wonders.**
B: Four wonders? What are they?
A: Odd pines, grotesque rocks, cloud seas and hot springs.
B: Wonderful, odd pines are unique. Are there some famous Huangshan pines?
A: Yes. More than 1,000 pines are named with different beauty and grace. Some of the most well-known pines are: the Guest-Greeting Pine, the See-the-Guest-off Pine, the Phoenix Pine, and the Black Tiger Pine.
B: The Guest-Greeting Pine is the most famous. **It always stretches out its arms to welcome guests all over the world.**
A: Besides odd pines, **the mountain's grotesque rocks are given fancy names such as the Flower of a Dreaming Pen, Monkey Gazing at the sea, and Turtle Peak.** Don't worry. I'll show you those rocks later.
B: Well, we won't miss them. What about the see clouds?
A: When on the mountain, you see clouds form at any time of the day. They float, stay, or spread. Their shapes change with each step you walk. As for hot springs, the water stands at 42 degrees centigrade all year round and is said to have curative effects for some diseases.
B: That's great. **Mount Huangshan deserves the fame for "No. 1 Mountain under Heaven"!**
A: It's true. There is a famous saying like this: **"One visits no mountains after the Five Sacred Mountains. And after Mount Huangshan, one has no eye for the Five Sacred Mountains."**
B: That sounds very marvelous and exciting.

Task 4

Listen and Answer

You will hear five questions. Listen carefully and give an appropriate answer to each of them.

(1) _____
(2) _____
(3) _____
(4) _____
(5) _____

Task 5

Role-play

Act out the following dialogs.

【Situation A】 Mr. Zhang is a tour guide who is going to show a group of tourists around Mount Emei.

Mr. Zhang:

- ☆ Reaches the foot of Mt. Emei and sees a big archway.
- ☆ Introduces the Chinese characters written on the archway: a famous mountain under Heaven（天下名山）; a Buddhist Holy Land（佛教胜地）.
- ☆ Takes the telpher to the Wannian Temple.
- ☆ Gives a legend about the Empeor Shenzong in the Ming Dynasty: renamed the Wannian Temple to express his gratitude to his mother.
- ☆ Tells that the beautiful view is called the Autumn wind over the Baishui Pool, one of the ten marvels of Mt. Emei.

Tourists:

- ☆ Get off the coach and take pictures.
- ☆ Want to know its characters.
- ☆ Ask for the reasons for changing the Puxian Temple to the Wannian Temple.
- ☆ Say it is a miracle and it is very kind of Emperor Shenzong.
- ☆ Appreciate the beautiful scenery: the maple leaves turn red all over the mountain and the red leaves are reflected in the pool.

【Situation B】 Suppose you are a tour guide to accompany Miss Smith to tour Mount Taishan. You are required to make up a dialogue including at least the following information.

- ☆ The highest summit 1545m above the sea level.
- ☆ Daimiao（岱庙）, the Dai Temple, the place where the God of Mt. Taishan is worshipped.
- ☆ Wudafu Song Ting（五大夫松亭）, the Fifth Rank Pine Pavilion, has a touching story.
- ☆ The Eighteen Bends（十八盘）, the 1,000- meter-long precipitous steps to the South Heaven.
- ☆ Gate.
- ☆ Yudi Feng（玉帝峰）, the Jade Emperor Summit, is the highest peak of Mt. Taishan.
- ☆ The temple of Jade Emperor（玉帝庙）.

Tour of Mountains   Item 8

Model 2
A Trip in Guilin 游览桂林

Task 1

Warm-up

Work in pairs. Discuss and answer the following questions.

1. As we know, the landscape in Guilin is the best in the world. What are the "Four Wonders" of Guilin's landscape? And what scenic areas are more famous in Guilin?
2. Guilin is famous for its beautiful scenery. Do you know which adjective words can often be used to describe the word "scenery"?

Task 2

Learning Points

Listen to the following *words* and *useful expressions* and repeat. Then try to memorize them.

Words and Phrases

landscape	['lændskeip]	n.	风景，景色；风景画
karst	[kɑːst]	n.	喀斯特
cobble	['kɔbl]	n.	鹅卵石
cormorant	['kɔːmərənt]	n.	鸬鹚，水老鸦
shroud	[ʃraud]	vt.	笼罩，覆盖
wonderland	['wʌndəlænd]	n.	仙境，奇异的地方
the Lijiang River			漓江
the Elephant-Trunk Hill			象鼻山
the Folded Brocade Hill			叠彩山
the Wave-Subduing Hill			伏波山
the Reed Flute Cave			芦笛岩
the Seven-Star Cave			七星岩
the Solitary Beauty Peak			独秀峰
the Nine-Horse Hill			九马画山

Useful Expressions

1. Guilin's landscape is second to none./ Guilin has the finest mountains and rivers under heaven.
   桂林山水甲天下。
2. Guilin's landscape is noted for its green hills, elegant rivers, strange caves and beautiful rocks.
   桂林山水以山青、水秀、洞奇、石美而著称。
3. To be an immortal is not as good as to be an ordinary person living in Guilin.
   愿作桂林人，不愿作神仙。
4. We are eager to appreciate the unique scenery with our own eyes.
   我们急切饱览别具一格的美景。
5. The water of the Lijiang River is so clear and pure that you can see the cobbles in the bottom.
   漓江的水多清澈，连江底的鹅卵石都可以看得见。
6. Fantastic! I feel as if in a wonderland.
   美极了！我好像置身仙境了。
7. What a beautiful sculpture of nature!
   多美的天然雕刻啊！

Task 3

Dialogue II

Listen to the *dialogue II* for the first time. Then practise the dialogue by reading it aloud with your partner. Read through it at least twice, changing your role each time.

A Trip in Guilin

A: a tour guide   B: tourists

A: Ladies and gentlemen, today we are going to tour Guilin, a world-renowned scenic city and an excellent tourist city in China.

B: Great. **Guilin's landscape is second to none.** Could you give us a brief introduction to Guilin?

A: Yeah. Because of a typical karst formation, Guilin's landscape is noted for its green hills, elegant rivers, strange caves and beautiful rocks. Guilin has the finest mountains and rivers under heaven. Some people even say, **"To be an immortal is not as good as to be an ordinary person living in Guilin."**

B: Marvelous. **We are eager to appreciate the unique scenery with our own eyes.** What are the famous scenic areas in Guilin?

A: They are the Lijiang River, the Elephant-Trunk Hill, the Folded Brocade Hill, the Wave-Subduing Hill, the Reed Flute Cave and the Seven-Star Cave, the Solitary Beauty Peak.

B: Which scenic spot should we visit first?

A: The Lijiang River, one of the most famous scenic spots in Guilin. Let's go.

B: All right.

(The guide and the tourists are cruising on the Lijiang River to Yangshuo)

B: Look! **The water of the Lijiang River is so clear and pure that you can see the cobbles in the bottom.**

A: Yes. The reflections of the hills in the water looks so real and the farmlands stretch out like green carpets. They form magnificent scenery on earth.

B: **Fantastic! I feel as if in a wonderland.**

A: Yes, the beautiful landscapes of Guilin have inspired painters for centuries. What's more, you'll enjoy another kind of fascinating view when you come on a rainy day. The hills are shrouded in mist. The water are clearer and the hills are greener.

B: There! The hill looks like an elephant. I remember seeing it somewhere.

A: It is the Elephant Trunk Hill. It looks like an elephant drinking water with its long trunk.

B: **What a beautiful sculpture of nature!** Look there. A fisherman is fishing on a bamboo raft and his cormorants are busy catching fish. What a fascinating scene!

A: That is a traditional way of fishing in Guilin. It is one of the things to attract tourists to Guilin.

B: I am greatly impressed by it.

A: Pretty soon we will see another wonder along the Lijiang River, the Nine-Horse Hill.

B: Why is it called the Nine-Horse Hill? Are there nine horses on it?

A: Yes, you are right. It is so named because there is a saying that if you are clever enough you can find nine horses of different shapes on the cliff.

B: I see. I try to be clever by finding as many horses as possible.

Task 4

Listen and Answer

You will hear five questions. Listen carefully and give an appropriate answer to each of them.

(1) _____
(2) _____
(3) _____
(4) _____
(5) _____

Task 5

Role-play

Act out the following dialogs.

【Situation A】 Miss Wang, a tour guide, answers some questions by tourists who have great interest in the Jiuzhaigou Valley.

Miss Wang:
☆ Confirms the tourist's opinion that Jiuzhaigou's waterscape is better than Guilin's.
☆ Says there are five wonders: emerald lakes, layered waterfalls, colorful forests, snow-clad peaks and Tibetan customs.
☆ Says that the tour includes the chance to visit the Tibetan villages.
☆ Tells that water is the soul of the Jiuzhaigou Valley and it has 108 lakes, 47 springs, 17 waterfalls.
☆ Says that all are fascinating, but the Nuorilang Waterfall is a landmark.
☆ Tells that tourists can see rainbows when the sun is shining in the summer.

Tourists:
☆ Think the waterscape of Jiuzhaigou is better than that of Guilin.
☆ Ask wonders to see in the Jiuzhaigou Valley.
☆ Tell that they have special interest in Tibetan customs.
☆ Ask which is the most typical.
☆ Ask which is the most beautiful one among plenty of waterscapes.
☆ Ask whether they can see rainbows above the waterfalls.

【Situation B】 A tour group is touring Lake Taihu. Please have a dialogue between a tour guide and tourists according to the information given below.

A tour guide:
☆ The tortoise Head Garden is the best place to appreciate the beauty of Lake Taihu.

Tour of Mountains   Item 8

☆ The place is like a tortoise sticking out its head into the lake to drink water.
☆ They mean the Tortoise Head Garden.
☆ The wind is not strong, and the waves are not big. If the wind is up, huge waves will roar.
☆ The lake often offers you a picturesque scene whether you look near or far.
☆ There are three hills or islands in Lake Taihu. The one in the center is called the Drum Hill. The other two are called the East Duck and the West Duck, because they are shaped like ducks.
☆ Let's go.

Tourists:
☆ Why is it called the Tortoise Head Garden?
☆ See three big Chinese characters, what do they mean?
☆ Hear the rumbling surging waves
☆ That should be spectacular.
☆ What a vast lake! How freely the birds fly!
☆ There are some hills in the lake.
☆ Can we go to the hills?

Model 3
Huangguoshu Waterfalls　黄果树瀑布

Task 1

Warm-up

Work in pairs. Discuss and answer the following questions.

1. Have you been to the Huangguoshu Waterfalls before? Where is it and what's special about the Huangguoshu Waterfalls?
2. Could you make a comparison between the Huangguoshu Waterfalls and a waterfall you have ever seen?

Task 2

Learning Points

Listen to the following *words* and *useful expressions* and repeat. Then try to memorize them.

Words and Phrases

rough	[rʌf]	adj.	汹涌的，吵闹的
thunderous	['θʌndərəs]	adj.	轰隆般的，打雷似的
roar	[rɔ:]	v.	咆哮，轰鸣
refraction	[ri'frækʃən]	n.	折射
arch	[ɑ:tʃ]	v.	拱起，变成弓形
float	[fləut]	v.	漂浮，漂流
gallop	['gæləp]	v.	飞奔
the Huangguoshu Waterfalls			黄果树瀑布
karst landform			喀斯特地形
the Water-Curtain Cave			水帘洞
the Milky Way			银河
the Rhinoceros Pool			犀牛潭
the Water-Viewing Pavilion			观水亭

Useful Expressions

1. The Huangguoshu Waterfalls is the largest waterfall in China, 78 meters high and 101 meters wide.
   黄果树瀑布高 78 米，宽 101 米，是我国最大的瀑布。
2. The Huangguoshu Waterfalls is listed in the national register of key scenic spots.
   黄果树瀑布列入国家重点风景名胜区名录。
3. The waterfall looks just like a huge curtain hanging in front of the cave.
   洞前的瀑布犹如一幅巨大的水帘。
4. You may feel bunches of pearls and silver chains are falling upon you.
   你会感觉到串串水珠，银色水链飞溅在身上。
5. What a grand and attractive scene!
   多么壮观、多么扣人心弦的景色呀！

Task 3

Passage Reading I

Listen to the short passage for the first time. Then practise it by reading it aloud by yourself.

The Huangguoshu Waterfalls

The Huangguoshu Waterfalls is the largest waterfall in China, 78 meters high and 101 meters wide, which is located on the Baishui River of Guizhou Province. The rough and rapid water of the Baishui River rushes down directly from the cliffs to form a nine-stage waterfall. The falls send out a thunderous roar which can be heard from long distances. When the sun shines over the waterfall, the mist appears changeably colorful through refraction of the sun.

The Huangguoshu Waterfalls is listed in the national register of key scenic spots. There are dozens of different falls, forming a picturesque view of karst landforms. The spectacular Grand Fall is the biggest in Asia. Its continuous flow of water varies in volume with the season.

Hidden behind the waterfall is the Water-Curtain Cave which dissects the Huangguoshu Waterfalls. The total length of the cave is 134 meters, including six windows, five halls and three springs. A road on the mountainside leads into the Water-Curtain Cave, where **the waterfall looks just like a huge curtain hanging in front of the cave.** Inside the cave, six windows let you view the falls from different angles; stretching your hand out of the window, you can touch the flying water. It looks like the Milky Way pouring down from the heaven. On a sunny day, a rainbow arches over the falls with misty clouds floating slowly over the valley. The Xiniu Pool, or the Rhinoceros Pool, 11 meters deep, is rhinoceros-shaped. The waterfall pours into the pool with the force of a thousand horses galloping. Standing inside the Wangshui Pavilion, or the Water-Viewing Pavilion, beside the Rhinoceros Pool to enjoy the flowing-down of the Huangguoshu Waterfalls, **you may feel bunches of pearls and silver chains are falling upon you. What a grand and attractive scene!**

Task 4

Listen and Answer

You will hear five questions. Listen carefully and give an appropriate answer to each of them.

(1) _____
(2) _____
(3) _____
(4) _____
(5) _____

Task 5

Oral Practice

Please give a tour guide commentary on the Huangguoshu Waterfalls in your own words to your partner.

Model 4
West Lake 西湖

Task 1

Learning Points

Listen to the following *words* and *useful expressions* and repeat. Then try to memorize them.

Words and Phrases

causeway	[ˈkɔːzweɪ]	n.	防堤
islet	[ˈaɪlɪt]	n.	小岛
boast of			自豪地拥有，夸耀
the Outer Lake			外湖
the Inner Lake			里湖
the Yuehu Lake			岳湖
the West Inner Lake			西里湖
the Lesser South Lake			小南湖
the Solitary Hill			孤山
the Lesser Yingzhou			小瀛洲
the Mid-Lake Pavilion			湖心亭
the Islet of Lord Ruan			阮公墩
the Ten Scenic Spots of Qian-Tang			钱塘十景
the Eighteen Attractions of the West Lake			西湖十八景
Spring Dawn on the Su Causeway			苏堤春晓
Autumn Moon over the Calm Lake			平湖秋月
Three Pools Mirroring the Moon			三潭映月
Watching Goldfish in a Flowery Pond			花港观鱼
Snow Scene on the Broken Bridge			断桥残雪
Orioles Singing in the Willows			柳浪闻莺
Twin Peaks Piecing the Clouds			双峰插云
Evening Bell Ringing at the Nanping Hill			南屏晚钟
the Leifeng Pagoda in the Glow of the Setting Sun			雷锋夕照
Locus in the Breeze at the Crook Courtyard			曲院风荷

Tour of Mountains   Item 8

weeping willow   垂柳

Useful Expressions

1. In heaven there is paradise, on earth Suzhou and Hangzhou.
   上有天堂，下有苏杭。
2. Thirty-six lakes though there are on the earth, the most famous one is in Hangzhou.
   天下西湖三十六，就中最好是杭州。
3. The four islands look like four glittering gems inset in the rippling green waves, adding an unusual charm to the lake view.
   这四个小岛好像绿波荡漾中四枚闪闪发光的宝石，给西湖增添了非凡的魅力。
4. It is said that the lake looks more beautiful in the rain than in the sun; in the dark than in the rain; in the snow than in the dark.
   晴湖不如雨湖，雨湖不如夜湖，夜湖不如雪湖。

Task 2

Passage Reading II

Listen to the short passage for the first time. Then practise it by reading it aloud by yourself.

The West Lake

Hangzhou is well known for the beauty of the West Lake and the landscape around it. The saying, **"In heaven there is paradise, on earth Suzhou and Hangzhou"**, is a fair reflection of people's admiration for this lovely city.

Su Dongpo, a literary master in the Song Dynasty, expressed his love for the West Lake in the following poem line, **"Thirty-six lakes though there are on the earth, the most famous one is in Hangzhou"**. In people's minds, the West Lake is a charming girl, simple and pure.

Lying in the west of the city and surrounded by hills on three sides, the West Lake is 3.2 kilometers from north to south and 2.8 kilometers from east to west. Two man-made causeways, namely the Su Causeway and the Bai Causeway, divide the lake into five separate water bodies: the Outer Lake, the Inner Lake, the Yuehu Lake, the West Inner Lake and the Lesser South Lake. In the lake are four islands: the Solitary Hill, the Lesser Yingzhou, the Mid-Lake Pavilion, and Ruan Gong Dun or the Islet of Lord Ruan. **The four islands look like four glittering gems inset in the rippling green waves, adding an unusual charm to the lake view.**

The West Lake boasts of its various beautiful scenic spots. Apart from "the Ten Scenic Spots of Qian-Tang" and "the Eighteen Attractions of the West Lake", the top ten famous scenic spots of the West Lake designated in the South Song Dynasty are as follows: Spring Dawn on the Su Causeway, Autumn Moon over the Calm Lake, Three Pools Mirroring the Moon, Watching Goldfish in a Flowery Pond, Snow Scene on the Broken Bridge, Orioles Singing in the Willows, Twin Peaks Piecing the Clouds, Evening Bell Ringing at the Nanping Hill, the Leifeng Pagoda in the Glow of the Setting Sun, Locus in the Breeze at the Crook Courtyard.

Walking or cycling on the Su Causeway is great fun. The weeping willows on either side of the causeway are pleasant to the eye. Standing on any of the six bridges, you can have a beautiful view of the lake, the hills and pagodas. In fact, the West Lake offers charming views all year round. **It is said that the lake looks more beautiful in the rain than in the sun; in the dark than in the rain; in the snow than in the dark.**

Task 3

Listen and Answer

You will hear five questions. Listen carefully and give an appropriate answer to each of them.

(1) _____
(2) _____
(3) _____
(4) _____
(5) _____

Task 4

Oral Practice

Retell the text in your own words.

Task 5

More Oral and Listening Practice:
【Listening】 Listen to the following passages and fill in the blanks.

Tour of Mountains   Item 8

Listening I

Touring Guilin

Guilin is primarily known for its charming and unique scenery. It has always been considered as _____. Many Chinese poets and painters, both _____ included, have been drawn to these parts, and they have all praised the beauty of Guilin _____.

Guilin offers tourists _____. Hills of Guilin are unique, which have been attracting _____ from all over the world _____. The hills have fantastically shaped peaks, studded with pines and small pavilions. So the landscape of Guilin has been praised as _____.

Listening II

Mount Lushan

Located in the northern part of Jiangxi Province, Mount Lushan faces the Yangtze River to the north and borders on the east with _____ _____ in China, Poyang Lake. The mountain consists of _____, the tallest being Dahanyang, rising to the height of _____ above sea levels. Altogether there are _____ in twelve scenic areas. The beauty of Lushan Mountain is attributed to its exotic peaks and mysterious caves, thunderous waterfalls and gurgling springs, ancient temples and stone forest, and buildings that seem to be suspended in midair. With this fantastic blend of mountains, water and cliffs, Mount Lushan is one of China's _____. Its beauty has been admired for centuries. About _____, Li Bai, a master poet of the Tang Dynasty, portrayed Mount Lushan in his poems, paying homage to the magnificent scenery he saw and enjoyed. He used this area as inspiration for many of his over _____. In 1996 Mount Lushan was listed as _____.

【Topics】 Divide the class into groups. Choose one of the following topics to discuss in each group. Give a short report about the group's opinion after that.

1. What kind of personal requirements do you think a hotel receptionist should have?
2. Beijing is facing serious sand storms, especially in spring and autumn. Do you think it advisable to move our capital to another city?

3. Do you like to eat out or prepare dinner at home? Give your reasons according to the suggested points.

   Eat out: avoid the boring processes of preparation and cleaning up; better flavor; variety of dishes; good environment; avoid quarrel or argument over chores involved with cooking an．d cleaning up.

   Eat at home: less expensive; enhance relationship; sometimes romantic; m．ore personal; enjoy cooking.

Item 9　Tour of Temples

中国庙宇

Model 1:
　　Visiting the Jade Buddha Temple　游览玉佛寺

Model 2:
　　Daoism　道教

Model 3:
　　Visiting the Confucius Temple　孔子庙

Model 4:
　　Visiting the Wudang Mountain　游览武当山

导游英语情景口语（第二版）

Model 1
Visiting the Jade Buddha Temple 游览玉佛寺

Task 1

Warm-up

Work in pairs. Discuss the following questions with your partner.

1. What are the main religions in China?
2. What are the Four Famous Buddhist Mountains in China? And where are they located respectively?
3. Have you heard of the Jade Buddha Temple in Shanghai? What is the temple most famous for?

Task 2

Learning Points

Listen to the following *words* and *useful expressions* and repeat. Then try to memorize them.

Words and Phrases

reign	[rein]	n.	君主的统治；朝代
destruction	[dis'trʌkʃən]	n.	毁灭，破坏
enshrine	[in'ʃrain]	v.	入庙供奉
burma	['bə:mə]	n.	缅甸
gold foils			金箔
meditation	[medi'teiʃən]	n.	思考，冥想
enlightenment	[in'laitnmənt]	n.	顿悟启发
recumbent	[ri'kʌmbənt]	adj.	横卧的
abbot	['æbət]	n.	方丈
Buddhist Master Huigen			慧根法师
Sakyamuni			释迦摩尼
Maitreya			弥勒菩萨
the Heavenly King Hall			天王殿

Tour of Temples Item 9

the Grand Hall 大雄宝殿
the Jade Buddha Tower 玉佛楼
cultural relics 文物
Dazang sutras 大藏经

Useful Expressions

1. I have some interest in Buddhist temples.
   我对佛教寺庙感兴趣。
2. The two jade statues are of great artistic value and are regarded as treasures of Buddhism in our country.
   两尊佛像具有极大的艺术价值，视为我国佛教珍品。
3. What kind of Buddha is enshrined and worshipped in this hall?
   这个大殿供奉哪种菩萨？
4. The Sitting Buddha is worshipped in the Jade Buddha Tower and the Recumbent Buddha is in the Recumbent Buddha Hall.
   坐佛供奉在玉佛楼，而卧佛供奉在卧佛殿。
5. The Sitting Buddha of Sakyamuni is 192 centimeters high and 1000 kilograms in weight.
   释迦摩尼的坐像高1.92米，重1吨。

Task 3

Dialogue I

Listen to the *dialogue I* for the first time. Then practise the dialogue by reading it aloud with your partner. Read through it at least twice, changing your role each time.

Visiting the Jade Buddha Temple

  A: Miss Ding, a guide B: Mr. Brown, an Australian tourist

A: Hi! Mr. Brown, we've arrived at our destination, the Jade Buddha Temple, a well-known Buddhist temple in Shanghai. Do you see the gate on the right?

B: What a beautiful gate! **I have some interest in Buddhist temples**. When was the Jade Buddha Temple constructed?

A: The temple was constructed to keep two jade Buddha statues in 1882, the 8th year of the reign of Guang Xu in the Qing Dynasty, and was rebuilt in 1918 after the destruction by the war.

B: Two jade Buddha statues? Could you tell me more about the statues?

A: Sure. In 1882 Buddhist Master Huigen brought five jade Buddha

B: statues to Shanghai from Burma. He had intended to ship the Buddha statues to the Putuo Mountain, however, because of the difficulty in loading heavy Buddha statues, two jade statues of Sakyamuni were left in Shanghai.

B: That sounds interesting. They must be precious.

A: Yes, They are carved with whole white jade. **The two jade statues are of great artistic value and are regarded as treasures of Buddhism in our country.**

B: Great. The classical buildings in the temple seem attractive and unique. What is the tall building in front of us?

A: It is the Heavenly King Hall, one of the three major halls of the temple. The other two are the Grand Hall and the Jade Buddha Tower. Well, we arrive at the Heavenly King Hall.

B: **What kind of Buddha is enshrined and worshipped in this hall?**

A: Maitreya, a laughing Buddha or the Cloth-bag Monk.

B: How about the Buddhas in the Grand Hall?

A: Three Buddhas with Sakyamuni in the middle.

B: Where are the two jade Buddhas worshipped?

A: **The Sitting Buddha is worshipped in the Jade Buddha Tower and the Recumbent Buddha is in the Recumbent Buddha Hall.** Let's go to the Jade Buddha Tower and visit the Sitting Buddha first.

B: All right.

A: Look. **The Sitting Buddha of Sakyamuni is 192 centimeters high and 1000 kilograms in weight.** It is covered with gold foils and decorated with many precious stones, which portrays the Buddha at the moment of his meditation and enlightenment.

B: Marvelous! The craft is perfect and unique. They are rare cultural relics.

A: Besides, more than 7,000 Dazang sutras are kept in the Jade Buddha Tower; these are all the invaluable culture relics too.

B: I see. Let's go and visit the Recumbent Buddha.

A: Here we arrive. Look, the Recumbent Buddha is 96 centimeters long, lying on the right side with the right hand supporting the head and the left hand placing on the left leg. The sedate face shows the peaceful mood of Sakyamuni when he left this world.

B: Wonderful. What about the larger Recumbent Buddha?

A: Oh. This four-meter-long Recumbent Buddha was brought from Singapore by the tenth abbot of the temple in 1989.

B: Thank you very much for your excellent introduction.

A: It's my pleasure.

Tour of Temples   Item 9

Task 4

Listen and Answer

You will hear five questions. Listen carefully and give an appropriate answer to each of them.
(1) _____
(2) _____
(3) _____
(4) _____
(5) _____

Task 5

Role-play

Act out the following dialogs.

【Situation A】 Miss Jiang is a tour guide who is taking a group of tourists around the Lingyin Temple in Huangzhou, a very famous Buddhist temple in China.

Miss Jiang:
☆ Says the Lingyin Temple is one of the most famous temples south of the YangtzeRiver.
☆ Tells that it located at the foot of the Lingyin mountain, near the West Lake.
☆ Says the temple was founded in 328 AD during the Eastern Jin Dynasty by Huili, an Indian monk.
☆ Says that the Lingyin Temple is mainly made up of the Hall of the Heavenly Kings（天王殿）, the Grand Hall of the Great Sage（大雄宝殿）, the Hall of the Medicine Buddha（药师殿）.
☆ The plaque（匾） that is put on the front of the hall was written by the Kangxi Emperor in the Qing Dynasty, the major statue in this hall is that of the Maitreya Buddha, or the Laughing Buddha. At the back is the Skanda Buddha, or Weituo in Chinese. On the left and right are the Four Heavenly Kings.
☆ The Grand Hall is three eaved and stands 33.6 metres tall. It houses a magnificent statue of Sakyamuni that stands 24.8 meters high. It is the largest wooden Buddhist statue in China, which was carved out of 24 pieces of camphor wood（香樟木）.
☆ Behind the main hall is the Hall of the Medicine Buddha, housing a statue of the Medicine Buddha.

Tourists:
☆ Ask for the location of the Lingyin Temple.
☆ Want to know the story about the original construction of the temple.

- ☆ Ask for the temple's major halls.
- ☆ Ask questions when visiting the Hall of the Heavenly Kings: who wrote the plaque that is put on the front of the hall? What is the major statue of the hall? Who is the Buddha at the back of the Maitreya Buddha? Who are the Buddha statues on the both sides?
- ☆ Ask questions when visiting the Grand Hall of the Great Sage: ask for the information about a statue of Shakyamuni.
- ☆ Ask for information about the Hall of the Medicine Buddha.

【Situation B】 Miss Zhao, a tour guide, is taking the tourists around the Asoka Temple（阿育王寺）in Ningbo. Try to make a dialogue between the guide and the tourists according to the following clues.

- ☆ It is under the Luhua Peak in Taibai Mountains, 19 kilometers to the east of Ningbo.
- ☆ It was built in 282 AD, so it is more than 1700 years old.
- ☆ The temple covers 80,000 square meters.
- ☆ It is one of the "China Five Buddhist Mountains, famous at home and abroad, and plays an important role in the exchange between China and Japan.
- ☆ It is famous for the Buddhist treasure: a bone from the top of Sakyamuni's head which is kept as a relic here.
- ☆ The Asoka Temple is grand in size with its splendid halls: the Grand Buddha Hall and the Hall of Stupa.
- ☆ On the Hall of Stupa hangs Emperor Song Gao Zong's inscription "Foding Guangming Zhita (Pagoda of Top Bright Buddha) and Emperor Song Xiao Zong "Miaosheng Zhidian (The Most Wonderful Hall).

Model 2
Daoism 道教

Task 1

Warm-up

Work in pairs. Discuss the following questions with your partner.

1. What are the Four Famous Daoist Mountains in China? Which province are they located in?
2. What does Daoism emphasize?

Tour of Temples   Item 9

Task 2

Learning Points

Listen to the following *words* and *useful expressions* and repeat. Then try to memorize them.

Words and Phrases

Daoism		n.	道教
confused	[kən'fju:zd]	adj.	糊涂的
Plato	['pleitəu]	n.	柏拉图
influence	['influəns]	n./v.	影响
individualism	[indi'vidjuəliz(ə)m]	n.	个人主义
emphasize	['emfəsaiz]	vt.	强调
excessive	[ik'sesiv]	adj.	过度的，过分的
philosophy	[fi'lɔsəfi]	n.	哲学
objective	[əb'dʒektiv]	adj.	客观的
subjective	[sʌb'dʒektiv]	adj.	主观的
impose…on			强加……给
external	[eks'tə:nl]	adj.	外面的，外部的
tenet	['ti:net, 'tenit]	n.	信条，教义
Confucius	[kən'fju:ʃiəs]	n.	孔子

Useful Expressions

1. Recently I learned a little about Daoism from the CCTV Channel 9, but I feel confused about it.
   最近我从中央电视台第九频道了解了一些道教知识，可是还困惑不解。
2. Lao Zi is considered to be the founder of Daoism.
   老子被认为是道教的鼻祖。
3. Daoism emphasizes strongly the union of man and nature.
   道教极力推崇天人合一思想。
4. "*Wu Wei*" is a central tenet of Daoism and has also been important in Chinese philosophy.
   "无为" 是道教的核心概念，在中国哲学中占有重要地位。
5. Who has greater influence on Chinese people or society, Lao Zi or Confucius?
   老子和孔子，谁对中国的影响更大？
6. In the Western countries Confucius and Lao Zi are the best-known Chinese philosophers.
   在西方老子和孔子都是最知名的中国哲学家。

Task 3

Dialogue II

Listen to the *dialogue II* for the first time. Then practise the dialogue by reading it aloud with your partner. Read through it at least twice, changing your role each time.

Daoism

A: Miss Fang, a tour guide   B: Julia Smith, a tourist from Great Britain

B: **Recently I learned a little about Daoism from the CCTV Channel 9, but I feel confused about it.** Can I ask you some questions?

A: Sure.

B: Who was Lao Zi, or Lao Tzu?

A: Lao Zi was a famous Chinese philosopher who is believed to have lived in nearly the 4th century BC.

B: That means he lived in nearly the same period as Plato.

A: You are right. **Lao Zi is considered to be the founder of Daoism.** He wrote the famous Daoist work, the Dao De Jing. His most famous follower, Zhuang Zi, wrote a book that had one of the greatest influences on Chinese, expressing the ideas of individualism, freedom, carefreeness

B: They deserve respect. What does Daoism emphasize?

A: **Daoism emphasizes strongly the union of man and nature.** It suggests that man control his environment not by fighting it, but by cooperating with it. One important tenet of Daoism is *Wu Wei* in Pinyin, or action that does not involve struggle or excessive effort.

B: That sounds interesting. Could you explain *Wu Wei* in detail?

A: OK. **"*Wu Wei*" is a central tenet of Daoism and has also been important in Chinese philosophy.** It means that man should act naturally upon objective principles instead of imposing his subjective judgment and thinking on other people and external things.

B: I also learned that Confucius was a famous ancient Chinese philosopher. **Who has greater influence on Chinese people or society, Lao Zi or Confucius?**

A: In my opinion, it's Confucius. Although Lao Zi does not have an influence as deep as Confucius does in China, he is still widely respected by the Chinese.

Tour of Temples   Item 9

B: There is no doubt about it. **In the Western countries Confucius and Lao Zi are the best-known Chinese philosophers.**
A: It's time for free sightseeing. Have fun!
B: Thank you very much.

Task 4

Listen and Answer

You will hear five questions. Listen carefully and give an appropriate answer to each of them.
(1) _____
(2) _____
(3) _____
(4) _____
(5) _____

Task 5

Role-play

Act out the following dialogs.

【Situation A】 Mr. Hu is a tour guide who is going to show a group of tourists around the Longhu Mountain in Jiangxi province. Make up a dialogue between the guide and tourists in accordance with the clues given.

Tourists:
☆ Ask for the location of the Longhu Mountain.
☆ Want to know for what the Longhu Mountain is well-known.
☆ Ask for "The Three Wonders" of the Longhu Mountain.
☆ Ask the guide for some information about Daoism in the Longhu Mountain.
☆ Tour the green hills and crystal water.
☆ Visit and know about cliff tombs.

Mr. Hu:
☆ Says it is sixteen kilometers away from Yingtan City in Jiangxi Province.
☆ Says it is famous for an Earthy Paradise of Taoism in China.
☆ Tells that the "Three Wonders" are the Taoism culture experiencing a very long history, unique green hills with crystal clear streams and springs among them, and the mysterious cliff tombs.
☆ Answers the concrete information: an important Taoism sect originated in the Longhu Mountain. In the middle of Eastern Han Dynasty (25 A.D.—220 A.D.), Zhang Daoling, the

first Heavenly Master settled down here and began to make Nine-sky Pills of Immortality. The Title of Heavenly Master Zhang passed on for 63 generations, witnessing a Taoism sect which experienced the longest history of more than 1,900 years.

☆ Tells more about the mountain and the stream: the mountain is the main attraction of the place and it has many strange-looking peaks. Luxi Stream, also called the Shangqing River, is well known in the area. The stream meanders through the mountains and it is pleasant to sit on a boat and enjoy the scenery along the banks.

☆ Tells some information of the cliff tombs: The Cliff Tombs here can date back to 2600 years ago, during the Spring and Autumn Period and the Warring States Period. Known as a natural rare archeological museum in China even in the world, the Tombs have attained a worldwide fame for their long history, large scale, rich antiques, and unique shapes.

【Situatiton B】 Miss Yao is a local guide. She is taking a group of tourists from New Zealand to tour Mount Laoshan in Qingdao, Shangdong Province. You are required to make a dialogue between Miss Yao and tourists based on the following clues.

☆ Mt. Laoshan is situated on on the shore of the Yellow sea, southeast of Shangdong province. The highest peak is 1,133 meters above sea level.

☆ It is one of China's major scenic resorts and has long held the reputation as "the No. 1 Famous Mountain on the Sea". It is a famous Taoist mountain boasting both mountainous and coastal scenery.

☆ The legends went that the first emperor of the Qin Dynasty (221—206BC) and the Emperor Wudi of the Han Dynasty (206 BC—220 AD) came here to hope to meet immortals, which gave a mysterious air to Mount Laoshan.

☆ The Taiqing Palace is the largest and oldest among the preserved Taoist establishments. First built in the early Northern Song Dynasty (960—1127), the palace has a history of nearly 1,000 years and features a simple architectural style. It is surrounded by countless scenic spots and is the center of the entire tourist area.

☆ The buildings of the Taiqing Palace are made up of "the Sangong Palace, the Sanhaung Palace and the Sanqing Palace". However, the whole style is very simple and clear. To be exact, the series buildings of the Sangong Palace include double three yards forwards and backwards. There are two very old cypresses in the Sanhuang Palace, which were planted in the Han Dynasty (BC 206—AD220). Another old rare camellia in front of the Sanhuang Palace has been lived over 700 years. In winter, around the Taiqing Palace, the trees are green too and different flowers are blooming.

Tour of Temples Item 9

Model 3
Visiting the Confucius Temple 孔子庙

Task 1

Warm-up

Work in pairs. Discuss the following questions with your partner.

1. What are your ideas about Confucius and Confucianism?
2. Have you been to Confucius' hometown Qufu in Shandong Province? What is Qufu well-known for?

Task 2

Learning Points

Listen to the following *words* and *useful expressions* and repeat. Then try to memorize them.

Words and Phrases

itinerary	[aiˈtinərəri, iˈt-]	n.	旅程，行程
Confucius	[kənˈfju:ʃiəs]	n.	孔子
venerate	[ˈvenəreit]	vt.	崇敬；敬重
sage	[ˈvenəreit]	n.	圣人，智者
disciple	[diˈsaipl]	n.	弟子，门徒
scholar	[ˈskɔlə]	n.	学者
prominent	[ˈprɔminənt]	adj.	卓越的，突出的
pillar	[ˈpilə]	n.	柱子
Oriental Holy City			东方圣城
architectural complex			建筑群
an imperial tablet "Ode to Xingtan"			"杏坛赞"御碑
the Confucian temple			文庙
the Apricot Altar			杏坛
the Dacheng Palace			大成殿

the Thirteen-Monument Pavilion 十三碑亭
the Kuiwen Towe 奎文阁

Useful Expressions

1. We are on our tour of Qufu, the hometown of Confucius and an "Oriental Holy City".
   我们赴孔子故里、东方圣城的曲阜旅游。

2. You will be seeing the largest Confucian temple in the world and one of the largest ancient architectural complexes in China.
   你们将看到世界上最大的文庙、中国最大的古建筑群之一。

3. They are the Dacheng Palace, the Apricot Altar, the Thirteen-Monument Pavilion and the Kuiwen Tower.
   孔庙的主要景点有大成殿、杏坛、十三碑亭和奎文阁。

4. The Dacheng Palace is the highest building in the temple and one of the three major ancient palaces in China.
   大成殿是孔庙的最高建筑，也是中国三大古殿之一。

5. The Apricot Altar is the place where Confucius gave his lectures in his later years.
   杏坛为孔子晚年讲学之处。

6. Yes, it was said that he had 3,000 students in all his life and 72 of them were more prominent.
   是的，据传孔子有三千门徒，七十二弟子。

7. In the Apricot Altar there is also an imperial tablet "Ode to Xingtan" written by Emperor Qianlong in the Qing Dynasty.
   杏坛里还有清朝乾隆皇帝所写的"杏坛赞"御碑。

Task 3

Dialogue III

Listen to the *dialogue III* for the first time. Then practise the dialogue by reading it aloud with your partner. Read through it at least twice, changing your role each time.

Visiting the Temple of Confucius

A: Miss Lily, a tour guide   B: tourists from England

A: Good morning, ladies and gentlemen. I am your tour guide and my English name is Lily. **We are on our tour of Qufu, the hometown of Confucius and an " Oriental Holy City ".**

B: That sounds interesting. Lily, would you please introduce today's itinerary?

Tour of Temples   Item 9

A: All right. Today we will visit the three attractions concerning Confucius one after another: The Temple of Confucius, the Mansion of Confucius and the Forest of Confucius. Our first stop will be The Temple of Confucius.

B: Thanks a lot.

A: Here we are. The Temple of Confucius is on your right. **You will be seeing the largest Confucian temple in the world and one of the largest ancient architectural complexes in China.**

B: The Temple of Confucius is grand and magnificent. When and for what purpose was the temple built?

A: In 478 BC, the year after Confucius' death, the king of the State of Lu had Confucius' former residence into a temple to venerate the sage. However, for centuries emperors ordered that his disciples and other famous persons be venerated here, too. Now the list is up to 172 scholars.

B: Yeah, what are the main attractions of the Temple of Confucius?

A: **They are the Dacheng Palace, the Apricot Altar, the Thirteen-Monument Pavilion and the Kuiwen Tower.**

B: What is this splendid building, Lily?

A: It is the Dacheng Palace, the core palace of the Temple of Confucius. The palace is 24.8 meters high, 45.69 meters long and 24.85 meters wide. **It is the highest building in the temple and one of the three major ancient palaces in China.**

B: Are the three golden Chinese characters "Dacheng Palace"?

A: Yes, you are right. They are written by Emperor Yongzheng in the Qing Dynasty. Have you noticed 28 stone pillars carved with dragons? Each pillar has nine dragons and the pillars are about 500 years old.

B: That's pretty old.

A: Ladies and gentlemen, here is the Apricot Altar. **This is the place where Confucius gave his lectures in his later years.**

B: Confucius had a lot of students, didn't he?

A: **Yes, it was said that he had 3,000 students in all his life and 72 of them were more prominent.**

B: He deserves the title of a great educator.

A: **In the Apricot Altar there is also an imperial tablet "Ode to Xingtan" written by Emperor Qianlong in the Qing Dynasty.** The ancient tree beside it is said to be planted by Confucius himself.

B: Thanks a lot for your commentaries.

A: You are welcome.

Task 4

Listen and Answer

You will hear five questions. Listen carefully and give an appropriate answer to each of them.

(1) _____
(2) _____
(3) _____
(4) _____
(5) _____

Task 5

Role-play

Act out the following dialogs.

【Situation A】 Miss Lily is a tour guide who is going to take a group of tourists around the Mansion of Confucius in Qufu.

Tourists:
- ☆ Ask for the location of the Mansion of Confucius.
- ☆ Ask for the area of the mansion and basic knowledge about the mansion.
- ☆ Ask for whether Confucius live in this mansion.
- ☆ Ask for the meaning of "Lord Yansheng"（衍圣公）.
- ☆ Ask for the information about the Grand Hall（大堂）.

Miss Lily:
- ☆ Says it's in the east of the Temple of Confucius.
- ☆ Says that the mansion covers 240 mu, and it has nine courtyards with 480 rooms, and houses can be divided into two parts: offices in the front and residences behind it.
- ☆ Tells that this is the living quarters for Confucius' offspring to live and it was also referred to as Lord Yansheng's residence.
- ☆ Answers the concrete meaning: it means the Duke of Yansheng, a title given to the descendant of Confucius by the emperor in the Song Dynasty. It is a hereditary title. In the Ming Dynasty an independent Residence of Lord Yansheng was set up, the yamen（衙门）in the front and the domestic household at the back.
- ☆ Tells that the Grand Hall as a public court of Lord Yansheng is featured by tiger-skin chairs, a giant seal, four necessities in the study etc.

【Situation B】 Miss Lily is a tour guide who continues to take a group of tourists around the Forest of Confucius in Qufu. Make up a dialogue between the guide and tourists in accordance with the clues given.

Tour of Temples   Item 9

Tourists:
☆ Ask for the location of the Forest of Confucius.
☆ Ask what they can see in the Forest of Confucius.
☆ Ask whether Confucius' tomb in the forest.
☆ Ask for the area of the Forest of Confucius.
☆ Ask whether there are a variety of trees in the forest.
☆ Say the forest is like a botanic garden.
☆ Say the forest is too big and ask whether they should explore it on foot.
☆ Ask whether there are some other famous persons' tombs.

Miss Lily:
☆ Tells that it located in the northern Qufu, about two kilometers from the city center.
☆ Says that the forest is the Confucius Family Cemetery, it has been the historic burial ground of the Confucius family for more than 2,000 year and members of the family are still buried there today.
☆ Answers the question: Confucius' tomb is in the center of the forest. After Confucius died in 479 BC, he was buried here. His descendents were buried at the same place. The place gradually grew into a cemetery with over 100,000 tombs and 4,000 steles.
☆ Tells that the Forest of Confucius covers an area of two square kilometers and it has become the largest family cemetery in the world.
☆ Tells that since Zigong planted the first tree for Confucius, planting strange trees in the forest has historically been viewed as an act of veneration and now there are over 10,000 trees in the forest.
☆ Tells the cemetery is in fact a forest and it is a good place to get relief from the hustle and bustle of the city.
☆ Says "no" and they can rent a bike just inside the entrance.
☆ Tells that Kong Shangren, famous author of the "Peach Blossom Fan" was buried here too.

Model 4
Visiting the Wudang Mountain 游览武当山

Task 1

Learning Points

Listen to the following *words* and *useful expressions* and repeat. Then try to memorize them.

Words and Phrases

cluster	['klʌstə]	v.	使……集中，簇拥
numerous	['njuːmərəs]	adj.	许多，很多
exotic	[ig'zɔtik]	adj.	奇异的，异国他乡的
homage	['hɔmidʒ]	n.	崇敬，致敬
miracle	['mirəkl]	n.	奇迹
represent	[ˌriːpri'zent]	vt.	代表，象征
exquisite	['ekskwizit]	adj.	精致的，精美的
advocate	['ædvəkit]	vt.	提倡，主张
gold-gilded		adj.	镀金的
foster	['fɔstə]	vt.	培养，养育
fossil	['fɔsl]	n.	化石
the Five Dragon Ancestral Temple			五龙宫
the Tianzhu Peak			天柱峰
the Golden Hall			金殿
the Taihe Temple			太和宫
the Southern Crag Palace			南岩宫
the Purple Cloud Palace			紫霄宫
the Yuzhen Temple			遇真宫
Wudangquan			武当拳
Zhang Sanfeng			张三丰

Useful Expressions

1. Clustering around the Tianzhu Peak are numerous outstanding peaks and exotic sceneries as if "ten thousand peaks are paying their homage".
   众多奇峰异景环绕天柱峰，形成"万山朝大顶"的奇观。

2. The large architectural complex includes 9 palaces, 9 monasteries, 72 cliff temples, 36 nunneries, 39 bridges and 12 pavilions with a total floor space of 1.6 million square meters.
   宏大建筑群包括九宫、九观、岩庙、三十六庵堂、三十九桥、十二亭，总建筑面积达 160 万平方米。

3. In December 1994, the ancient building complex of the Wudang Mountain was listed as the World Cultural Heritage.
   1994 年 12 月，武当山古建筑群被列为世界文化遗产。

4. A 10-ton sitting statue of God Zhenwu in the hall is an exquisite example of ancient Chinese art of copper casting.
   金殿内重达十吨的真武大帝坐像是我国古代铜铸艺术的精品。

5. The Daoist music in the mountain is also a living fossil of the music of China.
   武当山的道教音乐也是中华音乐的活化石。

Tour of Temples   Item 9

> ### Task 2

Passage Reading

Listen to the short passage for the first time. Then practice it by reading it aloud by yourself.

The Wudang Mountain

The Wudang Mountain is situated in Danjiangkou city in Hubei Province. Its main peak, the Tianzhu Peak, is 1,612 meters above the sea level. **Clustering around the Tianzhu Peak are numerous outstanding peaks and exotic sceneries as if "ten thousand peaks are paying their homage".** The mountain's scenic spots mainly include 72 peaks, 36 rocky cliffs, 24 streams, 3 pools, 9 wells, and 10 lakes.

As a treasure house of the nation, the Wudang Mountain is renowned for its magnificent and grand Daoist palaces, which are miracles of the world ancient architecture. The oldest temple on the Wudang Mountain is the Five Dragon Ancestral Temple which dates back to the 7th century AD. Most of the ancient buildings on the mountain were built in the Ming Dynasty. Being a Daoist, Emperor Zhu Di of the Ming Dynasty ordered 300,000 people to start construction in the Mountain for 12 years. The Golden Hall, the Taihe Temple, the Southern Crag Palace, the Purple Cloud Palace and the Yuzhen Temple were all built during this time. **The large architectural complex includes 9 palaces, 9 monasteries, 72 cliff temples, 36 nunneries, 39 bridges and 12 pavilions with a total floor space of 1.6 million square meters.** The palaces and temples in the Wudang Mountain represent higher standards of Chinese art and architecture during a period of nearly 1,000 years. **In December 1994, the ancient building complex of the Wudang Mountain was listed as the World Cultural Heritage.**

The Golden Hall on the main peak is a copper wonder. Built in 1416 AD, the gold-gilded hall is 5.5 meters high, 4.4 meters wide and 3.15 meters deep and is completely copper-cast, except for its base. **A 10-ton sitting statue of God Zhenwu in the hall is an exquisite example of ancient Chinese art of copper casting.**

The Wudang Mountain is the source of the Wudangquan (Taiji) created by Zhang Sanfeng. Wudangquan advocates the cultivation of morality and fostering of nature. **The Daoist music in the mountain is also a living fossil of the music of China.**

Task 3

Listen and Answer

You will hear five questions. Listen carefully and give an appropriate answer to each of them.

(1) _____
(2) _____
(3) _____
(4) _____
(5) _____

Task 4

Oral Practice

Retell the text in your own words.

Task 5

More Oral and Listening Practice:

【Listening】 Listen to the dialogs and fill in the blanks.

Listening I

Visiting the Jinshan Temple

A: Ladies and gentlemen, now we are at the main entrance to the Jinshan Temple.
B: _____?
A: Yes, that is true.
B: _____.
A: Sure. It is make up of several halls. Now let's walk into the forecourt through this gate. _____.
B: Why are so many tourists standing in line before the bell tower?
A: They are waiting for their turns to strike the bell, _____ _____. And bell-striking is one of the oldest Chinese traditions.
B: It seems the bell is made of bronze. _____?
A: It is centuries old. Please look at the four figures in front of you.

Tour of Temples   Item 9

- B: _____? They frightened me.
- A: They are four guardian warriors.
- B: I see._____.
- A: Exactly. Well, we are now in the Grand Hall. _____. It is always smiling.
- B: Yeah, who is it?
- A: It's Maitreya Buddha, also called the laughing monk.

Listening II

Visiting Leshan Giant Buddha of Sichuan

- A: Ladies and gentlemen, we've arrived at the tourist site of Leshan Giant Buddha. _____.
- B: What a magnificent Buddha! From this angle I could hardly see his head. The Buddha looks like a hill.
- A: Yes, it is. _____. There goes a saying, "The hill is a Buddha and the Buddha is a hill." It is the biggest Maitreya Buddha in the world.
- B: _____. How was it chiseled（凿出）out of the mountain?
- A: It was very hard to chisel Leshan Giant Buddha from the mountain. It was recorded that _____ to complete the huge project.
- B: Look, what are those on the Buddha's head? They look like stone balls.
- A: They are hair curls of the Giant Buddha. _____.
- B: Amazing! Look at his ears. They are so big.
- A: Right. Each of his ears is seven meters long. _____.
  Look down at his feet. Over 100 men can sit down on each of its 8.5-meter- wide insteps.
- B: _____. It's a marvel of the stone sculptures in the world.
- A: Now we have reached the feet of the Giant Buddha. Look up at the Buddha!
- B: Oh, we are all dwarfs（矮子）compared with the Buddha.
- A: Now you can take pictures in front of it. _____. Have fun!
- B: Thanks!

【Topics】Divide the class into groups. Choose one of the following topics to discuss in each group. Give a short report about the group's opinion after that.

1. Brief introduction to the main religions in China and their respective emphases on religious doctrines.
2. Name the Four Famous Buddhist Mountains in China and give an English tour commentary about one of them.
3. List the Four Famous Daoist Mountains in China and offer an English tour commentary about any of them.

Item 10　Tours of Historical Sites

名胜古迹之旅

Model 1:
　　A Tour of the Forbidden City　　游览紫禁城

Model 2:
　　The Tour of the Great Wall　　长城之旅

Model 3:
　　The Tianyi Pavilion Library　　天一阁藏书楼

Model 1
A Tour of the Forbidden City 游览紫禁城

Task 1

Warm-up

Work in pairs. Try to answer the questions below.

1. Why the Palace Museum is also called the Forbidden City?
2. Could you name the three main halls of the front part of the Forbidden City?

Task 2

Learning Points

Listen to the following *words* and *useful expressions* and repeat. Then try to memorize them.

Words and Phrases

anxious	['æŋkʃəs]	adj.	焦急的，忧虑的
imperial	[im'piəriəl]	adj.	帝国的
gorgeous	['gɔːdʒəs]	adj.	极好的
elaborate	[i'læbərət]	adj.	复杂的
exquisite	['ekskwizit]	adj.	精巧的
carving	['kɑːviŋ]	n.	雕刻品
terrace	['terəs]	n.	台阶
marble	['mɑːbl]	n.	大理石
crown	[kraun]	v./n.	使……成王，加冕；王冠
edict	['iːdikt]	n.	布告
feudal	['fjuːdl]	adj.	封建的
The Forbidden City			紫禁城
The Palace Museum			故宫
royal court			王庭
The Hall of Supreme Harmony			太和殿
The Hall of Complete Harmony			中和殿

Tours of Historical Sites   Item 10

The Hall of Preserving Harmony   保和殿

Useful Expressions

1. This is the world-famous Forbidden City where once emperors, empresses and their families lived.
   这就是世界著名的紫禁城,皇帝、皇后和他的家人曾经居住于此。
2. It was formerly used on such occasions as a new emperor's crowning, the emperor's birthday and the announcement of important edicts.
   以前太和殿是举行皇帝加冕仪式、黄帝做寿和宣布重要事件的地方。
3. It was here that the feudal emperors handled their daily affairs.
   中和殿是皇帝用来处理日常事务的地方。
4. Banquets and royal examinations were held here.
   保和殿是用来举办宴会和殿试的地方。

Task 3

Dialogue I

Listen to the *dialogue I* for the first time. Then practise the dialogue by reading it aloud with your partner. Read through it at least twice, changing your role each time.

A Tour of the Forbidden City

A: the local guide   B: the tourists

A: Good morning everyone. Now, we're going to visit the Palace Museum. Have you ever heard of it?
B1: Yes, but I only have a little knowledge of it. I'm anxious to have a sightseeing there.
B2: Everything is OK. Now, let's set off.
A: (An hour later) Now we are standing on the grounds of the imperial palace.
B3: Oh! It is so gorgeous and elaborate, indeed.
A: **This is the world-famous Forbidden City where once emperors, empresses and their families lived.**
B4: Yes, I can feel the grandness.
A: Let's move on.
B1: What exquisite carvings! What's that white terrace?
A: That's the marble terrace on which the three main halls of the front part of the palace were built.

B2: I'm eager to see.

A: Attention, please. This is the Hall of Supreme Harmony. **It was formerly used on such occasions as a new emperor's crowning, the emperor's birthday and the announcement of important edicts.**

B3: This hall is quite different from any of the royal courts I have seen in the west.

A: Yes, it is. Go ahead.

B4: Shall we proceed to the next hall?

A: Yes. Let's go on. This is the Hall of Complete Harmony. **It was here that the feudal emperors handled their daily affairs.**

B2: How splendid! The atmosphere here is so peaceful and tranquil.

A: The last of the three is the Hall of Preserving Harmony. It was built in the Ming Dynasty. **Banquets and royal examinations were held here.**

B1: Thank you for your excellent explanation. I learned a lot about China.

A: It's my real pleasure.

Task 4

Listen and Answer

You will hear five questions. Listen carefully and give an appropriate answer to each of them.

(1) _____
(2) _____
(3) _____
(4) _____
(5) _____

Task 5

Role-play

Act out the following dialogs.

【Situation A】 Mr. Tang is a tour guide who is showing a team of tourists from USA around the Forbidden City.

Mr. Tang:
☆ Greets the tourists.
☆ Introduces the history of the Forbidden City.
☆ Explains the marble terrace.
☆ Explains the three main halls.

Tours of Historical Sites   Item 10

Tourists:

☆ Want to know the history of the Forbidden City.
☆ Appreciate the grand scenes and want to know something about the white terrace.
☆ Express the anxiety to see the three main halls of the front part of the palace.
☆ Give exciting remarks.

【Situation B】 Mr. Jones, a friend of Tian Jun, comes to Xi'an. Tian and Mr. Jones go to visit the Terracotta Warriors. Tian was born and brought up in Xi'an and acts as a tour guide for Mr. Jones.

Model 2
The Tour of the Great Wall   长城之旅

Task 1

Warm-up

Work in pairs. Try to answer the questions below.

1. Do you know the Eight Great Wonders in the world?
2. Can you tell the story of "Mengjiangnv Weeping on the Great Wall" to your partner?

Task 2

Learning Points

Listen to the following *words* and *useful expressions* and repeat. Then try to memorize them.

Words and Phrases

ascend	[əˈsend]	v.	上升，攀登
construction	[kənˈstrʌkʃən]	n.	建设，建造
collapsed	[kəˈlæpst]	adj.	倒塌的
existing	[ɪgˈzɪstɪŋ]	adj.	现有的
crystallization	[ˌkrɪstəlaɪˈzeɪʃən]	n.	结晶
wisdom	[ˈwɪzdəm]	n.	智慧
photograph	[ˈfəʊtəɡrɑːf]	n.	相片

beacon-fire tower		n.	烽火台
invasion	[in'veiʒən]	n.	侵入，侵略
nomadic	[nəu'mædik]	adj.	游牧民族的
tribe	[traib]	n.	部落
breathtaking	['breθ,teikiŋ]	adj.	吃惊的
challenge	['tʃælindʒ]	n./v.	挑战/向……挑战
top	[tɔp]	n.	极点，最高地位

Useful Expressions

1. The construction of the Great wall started in the Zhou Dynasty in the 7th century B.C. and continued until the Ming Dynasty in the 15th century.
   长城的建造从公元前 7 世纪的周朝开始，一直延续到 15 世纪的明朝。
2. The Great Wall is indeed the crystallization of the industry and wisdom of the Chinese people and also a symbol of ancient Chinese culture.
   长城是中国人民勤奋和智慧的结晶，也是古代中国文化的象征。
3. The Great Wall was built to guard against invasion by nomadic tribes from the north.
   建造长城是用来抵御北方游牧部落的侵略。
4. Some people have walked from Shanhaiguan all the way to Jiayuguan.
   有一些人从山海关一直走到嘉峪关。
5. Each of the two ends of the Great Wall is called a "guan".
   长城的两个尽头均称为"关"。

Task 3

Dialogue II

Listen to the *dialogue II* for the first time. Then practise the dialogue by reading it aloud with your partner. Read through it at least twice, changing your role each time.

The Tour of the Great Wall

G: the guide   T: the tourist

G: There is a famous saying: "A man who has never been to the Great Wall is not a true man". Now we're going to ascend the Great Wall. Are you ready?

T: Yes, of course.

G: Have you heard of the story of Meng Jiangnv?

T: It has something to do with the Great wall, isn't it?

Tours of Historical Sites　　Item 10

G: Quite right.

T: Would you please tell us the story of it? We'd like very much to hear the whole story.

G: Sure. In the construction of the Great Wall many laborers lost their lives. Meng Jiangnv came to the Great wall with clothes for her husband only to find that he had died. She was heartbroken and wept so bitterly that part of the Wall collapsed. When she found her husband's body lying under the wall, she threw herself into the sea.

T: What a faithful wife. And would you tell us more details about the famous Wall?

G: OK. **The construction of the Great wall started in the Zhou Dynasty in the 7th century B.C. and continued until the Ming Dynasty in the 15th century,** taking altogether more than 2,000 years. The existing wall was built in the Ming Dynasty.

T: **The Great Wall is indeed the crystallization of the industry and wisdom of the Chinese people and also a symbol of ancient Chinese culture.** How long is the Great Wall? It is said you can even see it from the moon.

G: The total length of the Great Wall is about 6,000 kilometers.

T: It is beautiful, even better than the Great Wall I've seen in photographs. What are the towers on the wall?

G: Oh, they are called beacon-fire towers. You know, **the Great Wall was built to guard against invasion by nomadic tribes form the north.** When people found the enemy approaching, they would send smoke signals from the tower as a warning. When other guards in the nearby tower aw the signals, they would do the same. In this way, the signals would be sent all the way to the capital.

T: How clever the ancient people were!

G: Come on! Let's keep climbing up, the scene's even more breathtaking up there.

T: Has anyone ever walked to the end of the Great Wall?

G: Sure, **some people have walked from Shanhaiguan all the way to Jiayuguan.**

T: Really? That might be a challenge. What is a "guan"?

G: **Each of the two ends of the Great Wall is called a "guan".** Look, there are even people up there. Come on, let's have a race to see who can get to the top first!

T: OK, let's!

Task 4

Listen and Answer

You will hear five questions. Listen carefully and give an appropriate answer to each of them.

(1) _____
(2) _____
(3) _____
(4) _____
(5) _____

Task 5

Role-play

Act out the following dialogs.

【Situation A】 Xiao Zhao, a tour guide, takes a group of foreign tourists to the Great Wall. The tourists asks some questions about the famous wall and Xiao Zhao answers these questions.

Xiao Zhao:
- ☆ Greets the tourists.
- ☆ Introduces the story of Meng Jiangnv.
- ☆ Introduces the time of the construction of the Great Wall.
- ☆ Tells that it is about 6,000 kilometers.
- ☆ Tells that they are beacon-fire towers and their function.
- ☆ Explains the meaning of "guan".

Tourists:
- ☆ Greet the guide.
- ☆ Want to know the story of Meng Jiangnv.
- ☆ Want to know the time of its construction.
- ☆ Ask how long the Great Wall is.
- ☆ Ask what the towers are on the wall.
- ☆ Ask the meaning of "guan".

【Situation B】 The local guide is showing Mr. Davis around the Temple of Heaven. Mr. Davis is eager to know some information about the imperial temple and the guide tries his/her best to satisfy him.

Tours of Historical Sites   Item 10

Model 3
The Tianyi Pavilion Library 天一阁藏书楼

Task 1

Learning Points

Listen to the following *words* and *useful expressions* and repeat. Then try to memorize them.

Words and Phrases

pavilion	[pə'viljən]	n.	楼阁
equivalent	[i'kwivələnt]	adj.	等价的，相等的
combination	[kɔmbi'neiʃən]	n.	结合，联合
collect	[kə'lekt]	v.	聚集
posterity	[pɔs'teriti]	n.	后代
abide	[ə'baid]	v.	遵守
aggressor	[ə'gresə(r)]	n.	侵略者
missionary	['miʃənəri]	n.	传教士
chronicle	['krɔnikl]	n.	年代记，记录，编年史
architecture	['ɑːkitektʃə]	n.	建筑学，建筑业
elegant	['eligənt]	adj.	优雅的，精美的
flush	[flʌʃ]	adj.	丰足的，齐平的
gable	['geibl]	n.	山墙，三角墙
corridor	['kɔridɔː]	n.	走廊
rockery	['rɔkəri]	n.	为种植高山植物而造的假山庭园
kiosk	['kiːɔsk]	n.	亭
national defense minister			国防部长

Useful Expressions

1. The Tianyi Pavilion Library is the oldest well-preserved private library in China today.
   天一阁是中国现存最古老的、保存较为完好的私人藏书楼。
2. Never discard the books, and never take the books away.
   代不分书，书不出阁。
3. They are rich sources of local chronicles and imperial examinations and are precious

materials for the study of history, people, social customs and habits.

这些书主要是（明朝的）地方志和科举录，是研究历史、民情、社会习俗的珍贵资料。

4. It is not only world famous for its wide collection of books, but also for its unique architecture and elegant landscape.

天一阁不仅以其博大的藏书著称于世，更以其独特的建筑风格和优雅的环境而闻名。

Task 2

Passage Reading

Listen to the short passage for the first time. Then practise it by reading it aloud by yourself.

The Tianyi Pavilion Library

The Tianyi Pavilion is located in the west of Yuehu Lake in Ningbo City, Zhejiang Province. It was built by Fan Qin, a high-ranking official equivalent to today's national defense minister, during Emperor Jia Jing's reign in the Ming Dynasty (1368—1644). **The Tianyi Pavilion Library is the oldest well-preserved private library in China today.** It is a combination of culture, social studies, history and art.

Fan Qin loved collecting ancient books all his life, and his collection of books reached 70,000. To protect the books, Fan Qin made strict family rules that all the posterity should abide by the teachings of the deceased: **Never discard the books, and never take the books away.** However, many books disappeared as the years passed by. In the thirteenth year (1808) of the Jiaqing reign of the Qing Dynasty, books in the pavilion totaled to 4,049 in more than 53,000 volumes. During the Opium War, British aggressors plundered many books and sold them to French missionaries and paper mills. After many accidentals, books in the pavilion merely totaled 1,591 in 13,038 volumes in 1940. After the founding of the People's Republic of China, special management departments were set up to protect the Tianyi Pavilion. More than 3,000 volumes of missing books were found.

Now, the Tianyi Pavilion keeps a large collection of about 300,000 ancient books, among which 80,000 are rare copies including the woodcut copies and handwritten copies of the Song and Ming Dynasties. **They are rich sources of local chronicles and imperial examinations and are precious materials for the study of history, people, social customs and habits.**

The Tianyi Pavilion Library is called the "Book City of South China". **It is not only world famous for its wide collection of books, but also for its**

unique architecture and elegant landscape.

The Tianyi Pavilion has a flush gable roof, and is six bays wide and deep, with a corridor extending from the front to the back. In front of the pavilion is a pond that stores water for fireproof. Fan Wenguang, Fan Qin's great-grandson, rebuilt the pavilion by laying rockery around the lake, building kiosks and bridges, planting flowers and grass in the fourth year (1665) of the Kangxi reign in the Qing Dynasty.

Task 3

Listen and Answer

You will hear five questions. Listen carefully and give an appropriate answer to each of them.

(1) _____
(2) _____
(3) _____
(4) _____
(5) _____

Task 4

Oral Practice

Retell the text in your own words.

Task 5

More Oral and Listening Practice:
【Listening】 Listen to the following dialog & passage and fill in the blanks.

Listenin I

Visiting Mogao Grottos

T: My goodness, the Mogao Grottos have five stories.
G: _____.
T: Amazing! Some stand alone, and others are together. All are arranged in _____.
G: In the Yungang Grottos and the Longmen Grottos, statures are carved

out of rock, but here they are sculpted out of clay.

T: _____ ?

G: A local plant from the desert here was used to wrap the _____, and then clay was used for sculpture.

T: _____ .

G: Because the statues were painted. It's called painted sculpture.

T: Those_____ were really smart.

G: There is a _____ of murals in the Mogao Grottos, too. People believe there may be as many as 45,000 _____ of them. If they were put end to end, they would_____ a two-meter-high, 25-kilometer-long art gallery.

T: Wow, that's_____.

Listening II

Lao She Teahouse

Lao She Teahouse, established in_____, is named for the_____, Lao She, and one of his better-known works, "Teahouse". At the teahouse, customers sit in_____ drink the best teas in China, watch all kinds of_____, enjoy delicious traditional Beijing _____ which were eaten by Qing Dynasty emperors. Since it opened, Lao She Teahouse has_____many famous people from China and all over the world; _____the Teahouse is well known in _____ In 1994 former United States President, George Bush visited the teahouse. Other_____include former_____Kurt Waldheim and the Singaporean President, Wang Dingchang.

【Topics】 Divide the class into groups. Choose one of the following topics to discuss in each group. Give a short report about the group's opinion after that.

1. Can you list out the characters of Chinese tourism? (It may contain the scenic spots, the service, the unique products etc.)
2. Why do you think young people in cities like to hang out in bars?
3. Why does China enjoy a world wide reputation for her cooking?

Item 11 Tour of Chinese Characteristic Culture

中国特色文化之旅

Model 1:
　　Taijiquan　太极拳

Model 2:
　　Spring Festival　春节

Model 3:
　　Beijing Opera　京剧

Model 4:
　　China—Home of Tea　茶乡中国

Model 1
Taijiquan 太极拳

Task 1

Warm-up

Work in pairs. Learn the following words of Chinese traditional sports and games. Then answer the questions below.

wrestling	horsemanship	archery	kicking the shuttlecock
dragon boat racing		kite-flying	Wushu

1. Do you like sports and games? Why?
2. Which one is your favorite? Why?

Task 2

Learning Points

Listen to the following *words* and *useful expressions* and repeat. Then try to memorize them.

Words and Phrases

superior	[sjuːˈpiəriə]	*adj.*	上好的
internal	[inˈtəːnl]	*adj.*	内部的
circular	[ˈsəːkjulə]	*adj.*	循环的
coordinate	[kəuˈɔːdinit]	*v.*	协调
martial arts			武术（指功夫、柔道、空手道等）
in terms of			在……方面
concentrate on			全神贯注于，专注于
be superior to			优于

Useful Expressions

1. Taiji refers to the philosophic idea of the universe.

Tour of Chinese Characteristic Culture   Item 11

太极拳属于哲学的宇宙论。
2. Taijiquan features gentle and circular movements.
   太极拳以动作柔和和循环为特征。
3. Taiji is a sport that strengthens the body as well as the mind from within.
   太极拳是一项强壮身心的运动。
4. The most basic principles are concentrating on breathing control and the coordinated body movements.
   最基本的原理是注重呼吸的控制和身体动作的协调。
5. I'd be glad to.
   我愿意。

Task 3

Dialogue I

Listen to the *dialogue I* for the first time. Then practise the dialogue by reading it aloud with your partner. Read through it at least twice, changing your role each time.

Taijiquan

G: the guide   T: the tourist

T: What does Taijiquan mean? Is it superior to other martial arts?

G: Not exactly. **Taiji refers to the philosophic idea of the universe.** It is the continuous cycle of life.

T: How does it differ from other martial arts?

G: In terms of movements, **Taijiquan features gentle and circular movements.** It is especially different from many western types of sports in which the harder and quicker, the better.

T: How could you benefit from such a relaxed way?

G: **Taiji is a sport that strengthens the body as well as the mind from within.** It provides the mental relaxation. And it is known in China for centuries to be effective for some internal diseases.

T: That's why it is so popular, I should say. Is it easy to learn?

G: Yes. It is easy for health improvement.

T: What are the essentials for playing Taijiquan?

G: **The most basic principles are concentrating on breathing control and the coordinated body movements.**

T: Would you please show us how to do it?

G: **I'd be glad to.** Now follow me. You can also have a try.

Task 4

Listen and Answer

You will hear five questions. Listen carefully and give an appropriate answer to each of them.
(1) _____
(2) _____
(3) _____
(4) _____
(5) _____

Task 5

Role-play

Act out the following dialogs.

【Situation A】 Yao Tian and his foreign friend John are doing morning exercise in the Moon Lake Park. They find that a lot of people are doing Wushu. John feels it interesting, so he is asking Yao Tian some questions about Wushu.

John:
☆　Finds that a lot of doing Wushu.
☆　Asks why Chinese people like it.
☆　Asks what Wushu means and what about its history.
☆　Hopes to learn it.

Yao Tian:
☆　Tells John that Chinese people are fond of Wushu.
☆　Answers that people take up Wushu for physical training and self-defense.
☆　Says that Wushu is practiced in various types of set exercises, either empty-handed or with weapons, with its history as many as several thousand years.
☆　Feels glad to teach John.

【Situation B】 Talk with your partner about some traditional Chinese games that are played by Chinese children and adults respectively.

【Situation C】 Discuss with your partner about traditional Chinese sports that are played by the Han people and people of national minorities.

Tour of Chinese Characteristic Culture Item 11

Model 2
Spring Festival 春节

Task 1

Warm-up

Work in pairs. Think about the following question and discuss with your partner.

What festivals are popular in our country? How do we spend these festivals?

Task 2

Learning Points

Listen to the following *words* and *useful expressions* and repeat. Then try to memorize them.

Words and Phrases

terrific	[təˈrifik]	adj.	极好的
firework	[ˈfaiəwək]	n.	焰火
firecracker	[ˈfaiəkrækə(r)]	n.	爆竹，鞭炮
dispel	[disˈpel]	v.	驱散，驱逐
cuisine	[kwi(ː)ˈziːn]	n.	烹饪
speciality	[ˌspeʃiˈæliti]	n.	专长，擅长
dish	[diʃ]	n.	一道菜肴
feast	[fiːst]	n.	宴会，酒席，节会
chopsticks	[ˈtʃɔpstiks]	n.	[复数]筷子
considerate	[kənˈsidərit]	adj.	考虑周到的
prime	[praim]	n.	全盛时期
essential	[iˈsenʃəl]	adj.	必要的，本质的
Ningbo Municipal Government			宁波市政府
feast one's eyes on			尽情欣赏（艺术品）
work of ar			艺术品
take pictures of			拍照
remind sb. of sth.			提醒（某人）（某事）

to tell one's truth	说实话
the Spring Festival party	春节联欢晚会
stay up	熬夜

Useful Expressions

1. How did you spend the Spring Festival in China?
   您在中国怎么过的春节?
2. It is believed that …
   据说……
3. I really feasted my eyes on the Chinese food.
   中国菜肴让我一饱眼福。
4. I couldn't have the heart to eat it.
   我不忍心吃。
5. Thank you for saying so.
   感谢您这么说。

Task 3

Dialogue II

Listen to the *dialogue II* for the first time. Then practise the dialogue by reading it aloud with your partner. Read through it at least twice, changing your role each time.

Spring Festival

H: Helen (a Chinese student)　　B: Philips Bush (an American professor)

H: Happy New Year! Professor Bush, **how did you spend the Spring Festival in China?**

B: Oh, it was terrific. I was excited when I saw beautiful fireworks in the evening sky on New Year's Eve. I was simply amazed.

H: That's a typical Chinese traditional custom. **It is believed that** firecrackers and fireworks will be able to dispel bad luck and bring good fortune in the coming year. By the way, where did you have your Nianyefan, Professor Bush?

B: Oh, I was invited to a dinner party given by Ningbo Municipal Government. **I really feasted my eyes on the Chinese food.**

H: Really? In China, we have eight big cuisines, such as Beijing food, Shangdong food, Cantonese Food, etc., and in each cuisine, there are some specialties.

Tour of Chinese Characteristic Culture   Item 11

B: That's right. In my eyes, each dish was a work of art. It was so beautiful that **I couldn't have the heart to eat it,** so I took pictures of the dishes, which would surely remind me of the wonderful feast.

H: That's a good idea. But as I know, you can't use chopsticks well, how did you enjoy yourself at the dinner party?

B: To tell you the truth, the host was very considerate. And we can use either chopsticks or knives and forks, but I used chopsticks during the party. I think chopsticks are part of the Chinese food culture. If you can't use chopsticks, you will never understand the prime of the Chinese cuisine.

H: You are right, Professor Bush. Well, what else did you do after the feast?

B: Oh, after the dinner, we sit together, chatting and watching the Spring Festival party on TV.

H: Yeah, the Spring Festival party broadcast on China Central Television Station (CCTV) is an essential entertainment for the Chinese both at home and abroad. And according to the customs, each family will stay up all through the night, talking about the past and the future.

B: The Spring Festival I spent in China was a very pleasant experience. I won't forget it in my lifetime. I like China very much. If possible, I'd like to live here for the rest of my life.

H: **Thank you for saying so.** We sincerely welcome you, Professor Bush.

Task 4

Listen and Answer

You will hear five questions. Listen carefully and give an appropriate answer to each of them.

(1) _____
(2) _____
(3) _____
(4) _____
(5) _____

Task 5

Role-play

Act out the following dialogs.

【Situation A】 A guide and his foreign friend called Jane have just taken part in "The Mid-autumn Festival". They are discussing the festival together.

The guide:
- ☆ Answers that the custom can be traced back as far as the ancient Xia and Shang dynasties and it begins on the evening of the fifteenth of the eighth lunar month.
- ☆ Tells Jane that people like to send and eat moon cakes as gifts in expression of their best wishes of family reunion.
- ☆ Says that it is a traditional festival in China.
- ☆ Says that people will have a family reunion feast in the evening, while looking up at the moon to extend best wishes to their relatives and friends.

Jane:
- ☆ Asks when the festival celebration begins.
- ☆ Asks what people usually eat during the festival.
- ☆ Asks what kind of festival it is.
- ☆ Asks what activities are held during the festival.

【Situation B】You are going to spend the Lantern Festival with your foreign friends, who don't know anything about this festival. So you tell them all what you know.

【Situation C】You are discussing some traditional festivals of people of national minorities (e.g. the Water Splashing Festival) with your foreign friends. You tells your friends about the customs of these festivals.

Model 3
Beijing Opera 京剧

Task 1

Warm-up

Work in pairs. Think about the following question and discuss with your partner.

What forms of entertainment can be found in Chinese theater? Give some examples and try to describe them in details.

Task 2

Learning Points

Listen to the following *words* and *useful expressions* and repeat. Then try to memorize them.

Tour of Chinese Characteristic Culture   Item 11

Words and Phrases

appreciate	[əˈpriːʃieit]	v.	欣赏，感激
differentiate	[ˌdifəˈrenʃieit]	v.	区别，差别
elegant	[ˈeligənt]	adj.	优雅的，精美的
sleeve	[sliːv]	n.	袖子
encyclopedia	[enˌsaikləuˈpiːdiə]	n.	百科全书
monk	[mʌŋk]	n.	僧侣，修道士
disciple	[diˈsaipl]	n.	弟子，门徒
overcome	[ˌəuvəˈkʌm]	v.	克服
destination	[ˌdestiˈneiʃən]	n.	目的地
be composed of			由……组成
leave a deep impression on			给……留下深刻印象
stand for			代表
be regarded as			被……认为是……
refer to			涉及(参考，指的是)

Useful Expressions

1. But I have no idea about it.
   但是我对其一点都不了解。
2. It's my pleasure.
   我乐意。
3. It sounds very interesting.
   听起来能有兴趣。
4. Money Subdues the White Bone Demon.
   孙悟空打白骨精。
5. It will do me good to know something about the story in advance.
   事先知晓些故事情节对我有好处。

Task 3

Dialogue III

Listen to the *dialogue III* for the first time. Then practise the dialogue by reading it aloud with your partner. Read through it at least twice, changing your role each time.

Beijing Opera

A: Hi, Jack. Nice to see you.

B: Hello, Jane. Nice to see you, too. Are you free this Sunday evening?
A: Sure.
B: Good. I want to invite you to arppeciate Beijing Opera at the Grand Theater.
A: Great. I was told that Beijing Opera is marvelous. **But I have no idea about it.** Could you tell me something about it?
B: **It's my pleasure.** Beijing Opera is quite different from other performances, in that it is composed of all kinds of performances including singing, dancing, acting and talking, with very graceful music.
A: It's really great entertainment. Is it very popular in China?
B: Yes. It is called a national opera in China and also has become the most influential one both at home and abroad. Besides, it has left a deep impression on foreigners.
A: How about the actors and actresses?
B: The roles in Peking Opera are strictly differentiated into fixed character types: Sheng (male characters), Dan (female characters), Jing (painted faces) and Chou (male clowns). Their faces are painted in various colors, which stand for different characters.
A: **It sounds very interesting.**
B: Both actors and actresses are in attractive and elegant clothes with long sleeves which is regarded as an art.
A: I think it's a good chance for me to feast my eyes.
B: I hope so. By the way, I wonder why in Beijing Opera, males used to play the female parts.
A: I don't know. Could you tell me why?
B: Sorry, I don't know either. But I'll refer to the encyclopedia and tell you later.
A: Never mind. What's the name of the opera we're going to see?
B: **"Money Subdues the White Bone Demon".**
A: Could you tell me about it in details, otherwise, I'll be totally confused.
B: This is typical and traditional Beijing Opera. The main idea of the story lies in the close relationship between a monk and his three disciples. On their way to India, they meet many unexpected difficulties and the three disciples act differently.
A: What'll happen at last?
B: Of course, they overcome all the difficulties and successfully reach the destination.

Tour of Chinese Characteristic Culture   Item 11

A: **It will do me good to know something about the story in advance.** Thank you for telling me so much.
B: Not at all. I hope you'll enjoy yourself on Sunday evening. See you then.
A: See you.

Task 4

Listen and Answer

You will hear five questions. Listen carefully and give an appropriate answer to each of them.

(1) _____
(2) _____
(3) _____
(4) _____
(5) _____

Task 5

Role-play

Act out the following dialogs.

【Situation A】 Zhang Hui and his foreign friend Williams has just watched a masterpiece of Peking Opera. Now they are talking about Peking Opera.

Zhang Hui:
☆ Asks whether Williams enjoyed the opera or not.
☆ Tells the history, development and characters of Peking Opera.
☆ Feels glad to help Williams to understand Chinese culture.

Williams:
☆ Feels marvelous about the opera.
☆ Wants to know more about the Peking Opera, such as its history, development and characters.
☆ Expresses still puzzled about something.
☆ Thanks for helping him.

【Situation B】 You and your foreign friends are talking about Chinese opera and western opera respectively. They discuss the differences between them.

Model 4
China—Home of Tea 茶乡中国

Task 1

Learning Points

Listen to the following *words* and *useful expressions* and repeat. Then try to memorize them.

Words and Phrases

porcelain	['pɔːslin, -lein]	n.	瓷器
data	['deitə]	n.	资料，数据
beverage	['bevəridʒ]	n.	饮料
entertain	[ˌentə'tein]	v.	款待
process	[prə'ses]	v.	加工
jasmine	['dʒæsmin]	n.	茉莉
oolong	['uːlɔŋ]	n.	乌龙茶
fermentation	[ˌfəːmen'teiʃən]	n.	发酵
bake	[beik]	v.	烘焙，烤
partial	['pɑːʃəl]	adj.	部分的
border	['bɔːdə]	n.	边缘
compress	[kəm'pres]	v.	压缩，压榨
brew	[bruː]	v.	酿造
utensil	[juː(ː)'tensl]	n.	器具
flavor	['fleivə]	n.	风味
steep	[stiːp]	v.	浸泡，浸透
minimal	['miniməl]	adj.	最小的
workshop	['wəːkʃɔp]	n.	车间
be classified into			把……分成……
on the basis of			在……的基础上
in the course of			在……的过程中
comprise of			由……组成

Useful Expressions

1. …which makes China the homeland of tea, and the country that first grew tea, made tea

Tour of Chinese Characteristic Culture   Item 11

and discovered the effects of drinking tea.
……使中国成为茶叶之乡，第一个种植茶叶，制作茶叶和发现饮茶功效的国家。

2. Chinese tea may be classified into five kinds according to the different methods by which it is processed.
中国茶根据其不同的加工方法可以分成五类。

3. Green tea is made by firing tea leaves, keeping the original color of the tea leaves without fermentation during processing.
绿茶是由烧制茶叶制作成的，在加工的过程中同时注意保持茶叶的原先色泽，并保留香味。

4. The most noticeable ones are the making of tea, the way of brewing, and the drinking utensils.
最著名的就是茶叶的制作，泡茶的方法和茶具。

5. In order to let tourists have a better understanding of Chinese tea and tea culture, some scenic areas have preserved tea process workshops.
为了让游客对中国茶叶和其文化有更好的认识，一些景区还保存了茶叶制作工厂。

Task 2

Passage Reading

Listen to the short passage for the first time. Then practise it by reading it aloud by yourself.

China—Home of Tea

Chinese tea, together with silk and porcelain, began to be known all over the world more than a thousand years ago, and has always been an important Chinese export. According to historical data, China began to grow tea about two thousand years ago, **which makes China the homeland of tea, and the country that first grew tea, made tea and discovered the effects of drinking tea.** People throughout China drink tea almost everyday. Tea is also the most popular beverage to entertain guests in China.

In general, **Chinese tea may be classified into five kinds according to the different methods by which it is processed,** i.e., green tea, black tea, jasmine tea, Oolong tea, and brick tea.

Green tea is made by firing tea leaves, keeping the original color of the tea leaves without fermentation during processing.

Black tea, known as "red tea" in Chinese, needs fermentation before baking. It's developed on the basis of the green tea.

Jasmine tea is made by mixing jasmine flowers in tea leaves in the course of processing. Jasmine tea is well-known favorite with the northerners of China.

Oolong tea, a variety half way between the green and the black teas, is made after partial fermentation. It's a specialty in Fujian Province.

Brick tea is mainly supplied to the people living in the border areas of the country. It's so called because the tea is always compressed into a form of bricks, which is good for transport and storage. Brick tea is black in color, so it is also known as "black tea" in China.

Tea-drinking is an art in China. This art comprises of many aspects. **The most noticeable ones are the making of tea, the way of brewing, and the drinking utensils.** Tea is best brewed with water that has just come to the boil. It should be made in small amounts to keep the flavor from escaping. To make tea, porcelain pots are usually the best to use. The boiling water is poured over the leaves in the pot and the teapot is quickly covered to steep for several minutes. In this way, the fragrance remains there, and the tea tastes the best.

In order to let tourists have a better understanding of Chinese tea and tea culture, some scenic areas have preserved tea process workshops. Tourists can see various procedures of tea processing and even try their hands to experience how tea is processed.

Task 3

Listen and Answer

You will hear five questions. Listen carefully and give an appropriate answer to each of them.

(1) _____
(2) _____
(3) _____
(4) _____
(5) _____

Task 4

Oral Practice

Retell the text in your own words.

Task 5

More Oral and Listening Practice:

Tour of Chinese Characteristic Culture Item 11

【Listening】 Listen to the following dialogs and fill in the blanks.

Listening I

Traditional Chinese Festivals

A: Tomorrow is a _____ Chinese festival, the Dragon Boat Festival. _____ my hometown to eat Zongzi?
B: Great, thank you! Do you _____ the Dragon Boat Festival?
A: No. We have holidays at the_____, _____ and _____.
B: Are the holidays long? How many days?
A: Seven days for each of the three festival. My family _____ _____ during this year's Spring Festival.
B: Spring Festival is _____ in China, isn't it?
A: Yes, it is. It's _____ in your country.
B: What other traditional festivals does China have?
A: There are Lantern Festival, Mid-autumn Festival, Qingming Festival and so on.
B: _____ do you have at the festivals?
A: We have, for example, Jiaozi, Yuanxiao and Yuebing.

Listening II

Going to a Dragon Dance
看舞龙表演

A: Hello, Mr. Brown, _____.
B: Yes?
A: Would you please tell your _____ that tonight we are going to enjoy a Dragon Dance at Tianyi Square?
B: A Dragon Dance?
A: Have you ever heard of it?
B: Yes, but I think it must be scary to see a monster _____.
A: Oh, you're quite _____. China's legendary dragon is not the monster encountered in western mythology, but a benign creature symbolizing _____.
B: Really?
A: Yes. In ancient times, dragon _____ bring rain in times

of drought, _____ misfortune and bring good luck to all who need his help. This is why the dragon dance has become the most popular form of _____ at the _____ festivals, especially during _____.

B: It must have a long history then.

A: You're right. The custom can be _____ at least to the Han Dynasty some _____ years ago. Usually five to nine dragons danced together because in China the numbers five and nine _____ and nobility.

B: OK. Miss Lan, I will tell everyone in the group not to miss it. _____.

A: _____. See you at 7:00 p.m. then.

B: See you.

【Topics】 Divide the class into groups. Choose one of the following topics to discuss in each group. Give a short report about the group's opinion after that.

1. There are many similarities and differences between Chinese and western etiquette, can you list some examples?

2. Do you consider it necessary to protect our traditional culture, such as operas, folk music, arts etc.?

3. Chinese people entitle foods with symbolic meanings: People enjoy noodles which symbolize longevity on their birthday party; they sit around the hot pot in a circle, which represents happiness and reunion, and they will add some sweets, Chinese dates and chestnuts in the fillings of some dumplings to express their wishes. Can you cite more foods entitled with special meanings?

Item 12　Shopping

旅游购物

Model 1:
　　Chinese Calligraphy　中国书法

Model 2:
　　Antiques and Ancient Furniture　古玩家具

Model 3:
　　At the Souvenir Shop　在纪念品商店

Model 4:
　　Jade Culture　玉器文化

Model 1
Chinese Calligraphy 中国书法

Task 1

Warm-up

Work in pairs. Try to answer the questions below.

1. Do you know the Four Treasures of the Study?
2. Can you list out some famous calligrapher in ancient China?

Task 2

Learning Points

Listen to the following *words* and *useful phrases and expressions* and repeat. Then try to memorize them.

Words and Phrases

acknowledge	[əkˈnɔlidʒ]	v.	承认
treasure	[ˈtreʒə]	n	财富，财宝
stick	[stik]	n.	棍，棒，杖
slab	[slæb]	n.	厚板，平板；厚片
calligraphy	[kəˈligrəfi]	n.	书法；笔迹
innovative	[ˈinəˌveitiv]	adj.	创新的
parking lot			停车场
drive to…			驱车前往……
rich record with…			拥有丰富的……

Useful Expressions

1. As planned for today.
   根据今天的计划。

Shopping   Item 12

2. I expect the day for a long time.
   我期待这一天已经很久了。
3. What sort of things do they want to buy?
   他们想买些什么？
4. The most famous handicraft, that is, the writing brush, ink stick, rice paper and ink slab.
   最著名的手工艺品是：笔，墨，纸，砚。
5. Chinese calligraphy is a reappearance of this historic innovative process.
   中国书法再现了历史创新的过程。

Task 3

Dialogue I

Listen to the *dialogue I* for the first time. Then practise the dialogue by reading it aloud with your partner. Read through it at least twice, changing your role each time.

Chinese Calligraphy

【Scene】 Mr. Zhang, the local guide and Mrs. Smith and are driving to the Ancient Culture Street.
 A: Mrs. Smith   B: Mr. Zhang

A: Good morning, Mr. Zhang.
B: Good morning, Mrs. Smith. **As planned for today,** we are going to drive to the Ancient Culture Street.
A: Oh, **I expect the day for a long time.** Chinese five-thousand-year civilization and rich record with characters have been acknowledged by the world. Many friends asked me to buy some Chinese Ancient Culture things for them.
B: **What sort of things do they want to buy?**
A: A good friend told me that she hoped to get the so-called "four treasures of a study". Frankly, I don't know about them.
B: **The most famous handicraft, that is, the writing brush, ink stick, rice paper and ink slab.** Artists often use them to create the beautiful calligraphy.
A: I see. They are the tools of Chinese artists.
B: As we all know, in this long river of history, **Chinese calligraphy is a reappearance of this historic innovative process.** Many foreign friends coming to China are surprised at the tools when artists are creating calligraphy.

A: What time shall we set out?
B: Well, our car is waiting for us just outside in the parking lot. Shall we go to the Ancient Culture Street?
A: Yes. Please.

Task 4

Listen and Answer

You will hear five questions. Listen carefully and give an appropriate answer to each of them.

(1) _____
(2) _____
(3) _____
(4) _____
(5) _____

Task 5

Role-play

Act out the following dialogs.

【Situation A】 A tour guide is now introducing the Chinese Calligraphy to Mr. John.

Tour guide:
☆ Greets Mr. Jones.
☆ Says that they will visit the Chinese Calligraphy.
☆ Introduces the local Chinese Calligraphy shop to Mr. John.
☆ Offers information about the Chinese Calligraphy and its characteristic with its historic background in consideration

Mr. Jones:
☆ Greets the tour guide.
☆ Asks for the activity planned for today.
☆ Wants to know the famous local Chinese Calligraphy shop.
☆ Wants to know more information about the Chinese Calligraphy.

【Situation B】 A guide is introducing the Chinese silk handicraft (including it's history, how to make it, what usually drawn on it) to the foreign tourists.

Shopping   Item 12

Model 2
Antiques and Ancient Furniture   古玩家具

Task 1

Warm-up

Work in pairs. Match the words in column A with those in column B.

Column A	Column B
1. seal	a. 陶器
2. calligraphy and painting	b. 泥塑
3. teapoy	c. 印章
4. cupboard	d. 字画
5. clay figure	e. 茶几
6. Pottery	f. 橱柜

1. (   ).   2. (   ).   3. (   ).   4. (   ).   5. (   ).   6. (   ).

Task 2

Learning Points

Listen to the following *words* and *useful expressions* and repeat. Then try to memorize them.

Words and Phrases

coin	[kɔin]	n.	钱币
fake	[feik]	adj.	仿制的，伪造的
genuine	['dʒenjuin]	adj.	真的
reproduction	[ˌriːprə'dʌkʃən]	n.	复制品
mark	[mɑːk]	v.	标志，标记
look around			四处看看，随便转转
flower-and-bird painting			花鸟画
landscape painting			山水画
be marked down			打折

Useful Expressions

1. I want to look around first with my tourists.
   我想和我的游客先看看。
2. Shall I show you around and explain the antiques to you?
   需要我带你们看看并向你们介绍这些古董吗?
3. How about these ones?
   这些怎么样?
4. Their prices are very reasonable.
   它们的价格非常公道。
5. This can be marked down 20%.
   这个可以打八折。
6. You are a good bargainer.
   你可真会讨价还价。
7. But you will have to pay for the postage.
   但是邮费得自付。

Task 3

Dialogue II

Listen to the *dialogue II* for the first time. Then practise the dialogue by reading it aloud with your partner. Read through it at least twice, changing your role each time.

Antiques and Ancient Furniture

A: shop assistant   B: guide   C&D: tourists

A: Good afternoon, can I help you?
B: Good afternoon. **I want to look around first with my tourists.**
A: **Shall I show you around and explain the antiques to you?**
B: Thank you. What are these?
A: These are old coins of Tang Dynasty.
B: Ah, I see. And what is this?
A: It is lacquer screen with Chinese traditional paintings. Do you like it?
B: Yes. I like it, but I'd like to buy some paintings. Do you have good ones?
A: Yes. **How about these ones?** These are landscapes and these are flower-and-bird paintings.
B: They are beautiful. The horses in this picture are living. Who painted it?

Shopping   Item 12

A: Xu Beihong. He was one of the most famous painters in China.
B: Is it genuine?
A: No, it is fake. The real one is very expensive. All our reproductions are marked and priced. **Their prices are very reasonable.**
B: How much is it?
A: It is 500 yuan.
B: That is too much. I was born in 1954. My Chinese friend said that I was born in the year of horse. That is why I like this painting most.
A: All right, **this can be marked down 20%.**
B: Can it be marked down a little bit more? I won't take it until it is marked down 30%.
A: **You are a good bargainer.** All right, that is 350 yuan.
B: Can I have it shipped to the United States?
A: Certainly, **but you will have to pay for the postage.**

Task 4

Listen and Answer

You will hear five questions. Listen carefully and give an appropriate answer to each of them.

(1) _____
(2) _____
(3) _____
(4) _____
(5) _____

Task 5

Role-play

Act out the following dialogs.

【Situation A】 The tour guide is showing the tourists around the antique shop.

Shop assistant:
☆ Welcomes the tourists and the guide.
☆ Gives a brief introduction about the antiques in the shop.
☆ Gives vivid introduction about the things which the tourists are interested in.
☆ Explains whether the things are genuine or not.
☆ Offers the price.

Tour guide:
- ☆ Shows tourists around the shop.
- ☆ Asks about the things in detail of what tourists interest in.
- ☆ Helps the tourists in bargain.

Tourists:
- ☆ Ask the shop assistant to give a general introduction of what they own.
- ☆ Show special interests on certain things.
- ☆ Ask whether the things are genuine or not.
- ☆ Ask the price.
- ☆ Go bargain with the shop assistant.

【Situation B】At the antique shop, a tourist wants to buy a piece of ancient Chinese furniture – a writing desk. You are asked to help the customer to choose and buy what he/she wants.

【Situation C】At the antique shop, a tourist wants to buy some ancient coins. You are asked to help the customer to choose and buy what he/she wants.

Model 3
At the Souvenir Shop   在纪念品商店

Task 1

Warm-up

Work in groups. Learn the following words in the table. Then answer the questions below.

| wood carving | ivory | marble | bronze |
| crystal | glass | paper-made | fabric |

1. List out some kind of souvenirs that made by those materials above.
2. Can you provide other kinds of materials that can be used in making a souvenir?

Task 2

Learning Points

Listen to the following *words* and *useful expressions* and repeat. Then try to memorize them.

Shopping   Item 12

Words and Phrases

collection	[kəˈlekʃən]	n.	收集
recommend	[rekəˈmend]	v.	推荐
flavor	[ˈfleivə]	n.	味道
fragrance	[ˈfreɪgrəns]	n.	芬芳，香味
fascinating	[ˈfæsineitiŋ]	adj.	迷人的，极美的，美好的
miniature	[ˈminjətʃə]	n.	缩样，缩图，微型物
magnificence	[mægˈnifisns]	n.	壮丽，辉煌
exquisite	[ˈekskwizit]	adj.	精美的，精致的
scenery	[ˈsiːnəri]	n	风景，景色
craftsmanship	[ˈkræftsmən]	n.	技巧，技术
thoughtful	[ˈθɔːtful]	adj.	细心的，考虑周到的
a large collection of			大量的
be interested in			对某人或某物感兴趣
mind doing			介意做某事
to one's taste			合某人的口味

Useful Expressions

1. We have three major types: paper, silk and sandalwood fans. What kind would you like to see?
   我们这里的扇子有三种：纸扇，绸扇，和檀香木扇。你喜欢哪一种？
2. As for paper and silk fans, we have many patterns for you to choose from.
   至于纸扇和绸扇,我们有许多不同式样供您选择。
3. Do you want to have a look at each of them?
   每一种都要看看吗?
4. Shall I get you one from each type?
   要我帮你每款拿一个吗？
5. Ok, here are the fans you want and this is the change. Welcome to our store again.
   这是您要的扇子和找您的零钱。欢迎您下次光临。

Task 3

Dialogue III

Listen to the *dialogue III* for the first time. Then practise the dialogue by reading it aloud with your partner. Read through it at least twice, changing your role each time.

At the Souvenir Shop

A: the customer   B: the shop assistant

A: I know from the advertisement that you have a large collection of Chinese fans. I'm interested in Chinese culture. Can you recommend me some that have a Chinese cultural flavor?

B: My pleasure. **We have three major types: paper, silk and sandalwood fans. What kind would you like to see?**

A: I know little about Chinese fans. Would you mind explaining a bit more specifically?

B: OK. Sandalwood is famous for its fragrance. **As for paper and silk fans, we have many patterns for you to choose from.** Some are painted with Chinese calligraphy and poems, some are with historical figures and some are with oil paintings. **Do you want to have a look at each of them?**

A: Yes, please. (A moment later) Oh, amazing! How beautiful they are! I like them all very much.

B: **Shall I get you one from each type?**

A: No, thank you. These with paintings are especially to my taste. Is this Huangshan? The scenery is fascinating. And the oil painting on this fan is really a vivid miniature of Huangshan's magnificence. I'll take two of them for my friends.

B: You are really thoughtful. Here you are, sir.

A: How much are they?

B: It's 35 yuan for each. All together, 70 yuan.

A: Can I have a discount?

B: Sure, I will give you 20% discount. That is 56 yuan.

A: Good. Here is 60 yuan.

B: **Ok, Here are the fans you want and this is the change. Welcome to our store again.**

A: Sure, thank you, bye.

Task 4

Listen and Answer

You will hear five questions. Listen carefully and give an appropriate answer to each of them.

(1) _____

(2) _____

(3) _____

Shopping   Item 12

(4) _____
(5) _____

Task 5

Role-play

Act out the following dialogs.

【Situation A】 The shop assistant is talking with a foreign tourist about the wood carving which he wants to buy.

The shop assistant:
☆ Greets the guest.
☆ Tells something about the souvenirs in the shop.
☆ Tells something about the wood carvings' history and characteristics.
☆ Bargains with the customer.

Foreign visitor:
☆ Greets the shop assistant.
☆ Asks what souvenirs they have in the shop.
☆ Shows special interest in wood carving.
☆ Bargains with the shop assistant.

【Situation B】 You are a tour guide who is escorting the tourists to a souvenir shop in your hometown. You are supposed to help them in buying souvenirs.

Model 4
Jade Culture 玉器文化

Task 1

Learning Points

Listen to the following *words* and *useful expressions* and repeat. Then try to memorize them.

Words and Phrases

Neolithic DJ: [niːəʊˈliθik]   *adj.*   新石器时代的

archeologist	[ˌɑːkɪˈɔlədʒist]	n.	考古学家
excavate	[ˈekskəveit]	v.	开凿，挖掘
worship	[ˈwəːʃip]	v.	崇拜，仰慕
preserve	[priˈzəːv]	v.	保存，防腐；保留
exceed	[ikˈsiːd]	v.	超过(限度、范围)
merit	[ˈmerit]	n.	价值；优点
dignity	[ˈdigniti]	n.	威严；高贵；体面
utensil	[juː(ː)ˈtensl]	n.	器具
accessory	[ækˈsesəri]	n.	零件，附件
ritual	[ˈritjuəl]	adj.	仪式的
commodity	[kəˈmɔditi]	n.	[常]日用品
boom	[buːm]	v.	(物价)暴涨，繁荣
bestow	[biˈstəu]	v.	给与，授，赠，赐

Useful Expressions

1. Chinese first began to know and use jade in the early Neolithic period (about 5000 BC)according to archeologists and archeological findings.
根据历史学家与历史学研究发现中国最早于新石器时代早期（公元前5000左右）开始用玉。

2. Although other materials like gold, silver and bronze were also used, none of these have ever exceeded the spiritual position that jade has acquired in peoples' minds.
尽管也有使用金银铜等金属，但却没有一种金属可以取代玉在人们心目中的地位。

3. Until the Shang and Zhou dynasties, jade wares had been developed into tools, weapons, daily utensils, accessories and ritual utensils.
到了商周时期，玉已经被用来制造工具，武器，日用品，配饰和祭祀用品。

4. For thousands of years till now, jade was and is a symbol of love and virtue as well as a status symbol.
数千年来玉一直是爱，美德与地位的象征。

Task 2

Passage Reading

Listen to the short passage for the first time. Then practice it by reading it aloud by yourself.

Jade Culture

The history of jade is as the Chinese civilization. **Chinese first began to know and use jade in the early Neolithic period (about 5000BC) according**

Shopping   Item 12

to **archeologists and archeological findings**, represented by the Hemudu culture in Zhejiang province, and from the middle and late Neolithic period, represented by the Hongshan culture along the Lao river, the Longshan culture along the Yellow River, and the Yangshao culture in the Tai lake region.

Many jade wares dating back to 4,000 to 6,000 years ago have been excavated in different places. It changed from the use of decoration into the others such as the rites of worship and burial. Jade was believed to have the function of preserving the body after death and can be found in emperors' tombs from thousands of years ago. One tomb contained an entire suit made out of jade, to assure the physical immortality of its owner. **Although other materials like gold, silver and bronze were also used, none of these have ever exceeded the spiritual position that jade has acquired in peoples' minds**——it is associated with merit, morality, grace and dignity.

Until the Shang and Zhou dynasties, jade wares had been developed into tools, weapons, daily utensils, accessories and ritual utensils. As commodity exchange boomed, jade was bestowed with currency function. **For thousands of years till now, jade was and is a symbol of love and virtue as well as a status symbol.**

Task 3

Listen and Answer

You will hear five questions. Listen carefully and give an appropriate answer to each of them.
(1) _____
(2) _____
(3) _____
(4) _____
(5) _____

Task 4

Oral Practice

Retell the text in your own words.

Task 5

More Oral and Listening Practice:

【Listening】 Listen to the dialogs and fill in the blanks.

Listening I

At the Jewelry's Store

A: Can I help you, madam?
B: Yes, I'd like _____ for my friends.
A: Would you like jewelry? Today is _____ and all the jewelry is on sale at Rich's store.
B: That's great. _____ jewels?
A: Yes, we have 24K and _____ gold necklaces, chain and earrings.
B: May I have a look?
A: Sure. _____. Its regular price is_____, and now you can have it with a twenty percent discount.
B: It's very elegant. _____.
A: All right. Is there anything else you want?
B: Will you show me that _____?
A: Yes, here you are.

Listening II

At the Shop

A: Good morning, sir. May I help you?
B: Yes, can you _____?
A: How about some dolls? Girls that age are especially_____.
B: She has already got plenty of dolls. I'd like to _____ _____ this time.
A: Maybe you can buy her a watch. You see, I have a _____of watches.
B: This is a good idea. Can you _____ for me?
A: This kind of watch is _____. It's very popular among children. Furthermore, the _____and it is cheap too.
B: I suppose my daughter will like it. _____?
A: 25 dollars.
B: Well, could you wrap it up for me?
A: Certainly. I'm sure your daughter _____ watch.
B: Thank you.
A: You're welcome.

【Topics】 Divide the class into groups. Choose one of the following topics to discuss in each

Shopping   Item 12

group. Give a short report about the group's opinion after that.

1. Why can't the poor people benefit from the development of tourism?
2. In which aspect do you think we should improve to set up a perfect tourism market?
3. Do you think it worthwhile to protect cultural relics? Why?

Item 13 Handling Problems & Emergencies

处理问题与紧急情况

Model 1:
    A Lost Passport　遗失护照

Model 2:
    Calling the First Aid Center　打电话到急救中心

Model 3:
    First Aid Techniques　急救技术

Handling Problems & Emergencies   Item 13

Model 1
A Lost Passport 遗失护照

Task 1

Warm-up

Work in pairs. Try to list out the most possible place that the foreign visitor may leave his/her passport in or at.

Task 2

Learning Points

Listen to the following *words* and *useful expressions* and repeat. Then try to memorize them.

Words and Phrases

passport	['pɑːspɔːt]	n.	护照
vehicle	['viːikl]	n.	机动车
contact	['kɔntækt]	v.	联系
contact with…			与某人或某物联系
find out			找到
belong to			属于

Useful Expressions

1. Are you sure you've lost it?
   你确定已经遗失了吗?
2. Have you looked in every possible place that you may have left it?
   你是否已经在每个可能的地方都找过了?
3. Have you taken any taxis today?
   你今天有没有乘坐任何交通工具?
4. Can you remember the taxi's car number?
   你能否记起车牌号码?

5. And after that we may contact with the driver to get back your passport.
   然后我们可以和司机联系以取回你的护照。
6. It's my job.
   这是我的职责所在。

Task 3

Dialogue I

Listen to the *dialogue I* for the first time. Then practise the dialogue by reading it aloud with your partner. Read through it at least twice, changing your role each time.

A Lost Passport

A: visitor   B: tour guide

A: I think I have lost my passport.
B: That's a serious problem. **Are you sure you've lost it?**
A: I'm afraid so.
B: **Have you looked in every possible place that you may have left it?**
A: I have searched every place that I can think about.
B: **Have you taken any taxis today?**
A: Yes, I've taken a taxi 2 hours ago. Oh my god, I may leave it on the taxi.
B: Don't worry. **Can you remember the taxi's car number?**
A: I'm afraid I can't. But I can recall its color. It's green.
B: Ok, then, we may find out which company it belongs to. **And after that we may contact with the driver to get back your passport.**
A: I hope so, thank you for your help.
B: **It's my job.** Now, let's try to find out the driver.

Task 4

Listen and Answer

You will hear five questions. Listen carefully and give an appropriate answer to each of them.

(1) _____
(2) _____
(3) _____

Handling Problems & Emergencies   Item 13

(4) _____
(5) _____

Task 5

Role-play

Act out the following dialogs.

【Situation A】 After leaving the hotel, a foreign visitor found that her passport is lost. She is now asking help from the tour guide for the lost passport.

The visitor:
☆ Announces the missing of her passport.
☆ Declares that she has found everywhere.
☆ Remembers that she may leave it in the hotel.

The tour guide:
☆ Makes confirmation that the passport is really lost.
☆ Asks whether the visitor has already searched every possible place.
☆ Reminds the visitor whether she has left it in the hotel.
☆ Promises that he will help the visitor to get back the passport.
☆ Says that it's his duty to help the visitor to solve problem.

【Situation B】 At the bus station, a tourist found that his ID card had lost and he/she needs your help. (The ID card may left in a restaurant they had just have a dinner there)

Model 2
Calling the First Aid Center   打电话到急救中心

Task 1

Warm-up

Work in pairs. Learn the following words and answer the question below.

ache	bleed	faint	influenza	diarrhea
dispensary	blood bank	out-patient department		
in-patient department	registration office			

What will you do if the tourists get ill in the trip?

Task 2

Learning Points

Listen to the following *words* and *useful expressions* and repeat. Then try to memorize them.

Words and Phrases

ambulance	[ˈæmbjuləns]	n.	救护车
urgent	[ˈəːʒənt]	adj.	紧急的
cute	[kjuːt]	adj.	急性的
appendicitis	[əˌpendiˈsaitis]	n.	阑尾炎
stretcher	[ˈstretʃə]	n.	担架
bathe	[beið]	n.	清洗，洗澡
remove	[riˈmuːv]	v.	移除
right away			立即，马上
suffer from			承受痛苦
emergency ward			急救室

Useful Expressions

1. Please send an ambulance to 68 Hu Nan Road.
   请派一辆救护车到湖南路 68 号。
2. I think the patient is suffering from a cute appendicitis.
   我认为病人可能得了急性阑尾炎。
3. He's very ill.
   他病得很厉害。
4. What's the trouble with him, doctor?
   他到底怎么了？
5. When could I take care of him?
   我什么时候可以照顾他？

Task 3

Dialogue II

Listen to the *dialogue II* for the first time. Then practise the dialogue by reading it aloud with your partner. Read through it at least twice, changing your role each time.

Handling Problems & Emergencies Item 13

Calling the First Aid Center

【Scene】 *A foreign visitor is suffering from a cute appendicitis. Now the tour guide is calling the first aid center for help.*

     T: tour guide H: hospital receiver D: doctor

T: Is this the Friendship Hospital? **Please send an ambulance to 68 Hu Nan Road.**

H: Is it urgent? Our ambulances are not enough to meet every call.

T: Of course. It's urgent. **I think the patient is suffering from a cute appendicitis.** He may die if not treated in time.

H: All right, we'll come right away.

  (after a while…)

H: Where's the patient?

T: He's there in the room. **He's very ill.**

H: Don't worry. We'll put him in the stretcher. You are coming with us? Step in please.

D: Carry him into the emergency ward. Here we are.

T: I'm his guide. **What's the trouble with him, doctor?**

D: He had appendicitis, but is all right now that it was removed. He'll have to rest for a few weeks to recover.

T: May I send food for him?

D: No, outside food is not permitted.

T: **When could I take care of him?**

D: Our nurse can take good care of him.

Task 4

Listen and Answer

You will hear five questions. Listen carefully and give an appropriate answer to each of them.

(1) _____

(2) _____

(3) _____

(4) _____

(5) _____

Task 5

Role-play

Act out the following dialogs.

【Situation A】 You are an English tour guide who is calling the first aid center for a medical care of an ill tourist.

Tour guide:
- ☆ Calls the first aid center.
- ☆ Asks them to send an ambulance.
- ☆ Tells them that the patient is very ill.
- ☆ Asks when can take care of the patient again.

Hospital receiver:
- ☆ Answers the phone.
- ☆ Explains that the ambulance is in short number.
- ☆ Tells the guide that they will sent one.
- ☆ Asks for the accurate address.

Doctor:
- ☆ Does preparation work.
- ☆ Asks the guide to go with him.
- ☆ Confirms the patient's situation.
- ☆ Responds to the guide's requirement.

【Situation B】 One of your tourists has got a diarrhea, you should call the first aid center for help.

【Situation C】 One of your tourists has got a bad wound and bleeding heavily, you should call the first aid center for help.

Model 3
First Aid Techniques 急救技术

Task 1

Learning Points

Listen to the following *words* and *useful expressions* and repeat. Then try to memorize them.

Handling Problems & Emergencies   Item 13

Words and Phrases

climate	[ˈklaimət]	n.	气候
zone	[zəun]	n.	区域，范围
artificial	[ˌɑːtiˈfiʃəl]	adj.	人工的
respiration	[ˌrespiˈreiʃn]	n.	呼吸
straightly	[streitli]	adv.	笔直地
thumb	[θʌm]	n.	拇指
forefinger	[ˈfɔː,fiŋgə]	n.	食指
nip	[nip]	v.	夹，捏
inhale	[inˈheil]	v.	吸气

Useful Expressions

1. Changes in climate and time zone, long hours of sightseeing may easily cause such kind of sudden heart attack .
   气候的变化，时区的更迭以及长时间的观光很容易引发各类心脏疾病。
2. The most common use of FATs (First Aid Techniques) is Artificial Respiration.
   最常见的急救技术是人工呼吸。
3. Use thumb and forefinger to nip the wing of nose.
   用拇指与食指夹住鼻子。
4. After a deep inhale of air, the operator should cover the patient's mouth with his own lips and put the air in to the patient's mouth slowly.
   深吸一口气，然后急救人员用嘴将空气缓缓输入到病人的口腔里。
5. Do it for several times and with each time no more than 1 to 1.5 seconds.
   重复数次，间隔不超过 1 到 1.5 秒。

Task 2

Passage Reading

Listen to the short passage for the first time. Then practise it by reading it aloud by yourself.

First Aid Techniques

Changes in climate and time zone, long hours of sightseeing may easily cause such kind of sudden heart attack. In order to save the tourist's life at first time, you should know how to give first aid to him/her. **The most common use of FATs (First Aid Techniques) is Artificial Respiration.** It can be operated easily in any condition.

As for artificial respiration, you should first let the patient lay on a flat ground straightly. And also you should put his arms close to his body. Then, clean his mouth. After all these preparation works finished, you can do it now. **Use thumb and forefinger to nip the wing of nose. After a deep inhale of air, the operator should cover the patient's mouth with his own lips and put the air in to the patient's mouth slowly.** And make sure that the air goes in to the patient's body. **Do it for several times and with each time no more than 1 to 1.5 seconds.**

Task 3

Listen and Answer

You will hear five questions. Listen carefully and give an appropriate answer to each of them.
(1) _____
(2) _____
(3) _____
(4) _____
(5) _____

Task 4

Oral Practice

Retell the text in your own words.

Task 5

More Oral and Listening Practice:
【Listening】 Listen to the dialogs and fill in the blanks.

Listening I

The Lost Passport

A: U.S. Embassy in Stockholm. May I help you?
B: Hello? My name is Kathy. I'm an American citizen. _____.
A: _____, young lady. Are you sure you've lost it?

Handling Problems & Emergencies   Item 13

B: I'm afraid so. _____, what can I do?
A: If you can't find it, _____ to the embassy to the passport section. You'll have to _____ and pay for a replacement.
B: I have your address, but I don't know _____.
A: The passport section is open on weekdays from _____ and on Saturdays from _____.
B: Well, thanks a lot.
A: You're welcome. And _____!

Listening II

About Toilet

A: Maintenance Department. Can I help you?
B: Yes, there seems to be _____ with the toilet.
A: We'll send someone to repair it immediately. _____?
B: _____.
A: May I come in?
B: Come in.
A: The _____ doesn't flush.
B: Let me see. Oh, it's clogged... It's _____ now. You may try it.
A: Yes, it's working now. Thank you.
B: You're welcome. _____?
A: _____. I can hardly sleep.
B: I'm very sorry, sir. Some part needs to be _____. I will be back soon.

【Topics】 Divide the class into groups. Choose one of the following topics to discuss in each group. Give a short report about the group's opinion after that.

1. What's a guide's responsibility in facing with the emergent situation that happened to a tourist?
2. How to prevent the guests from being troubled by emergent situation?
3. The Chinese wine culture is closely related to all kinds of social activities. List some examples to demonstrate the relationship.

Item 14 Handling Customer Complaints

顾客投诉处理服务

Model 1:
   A Delayed Flight   航班延误

Model 2:
   Complaining about the food   食品投诉

Model 3:
   A Tour Guide or a Shopping Guide   导游还是导购

Model 4:
   A Complaint Letter on Holiday Booking
   旅游度假投诉信

Handling Customer Complaints Item 14

Model 1
A Delayed Flight 航班延误

Task 1

Warm-up

Work in pairs. Discuss which would be the most headache problem that a tour guide may face with according to the stations given below and why?

1. Tourists complaining about the trip.
2. Tourists complaining about the food and the guest room.
3. Tourists complaining about the delayed transportations.
4. Tourists complaining about the shopping arrangement.

Task 2

Learning Points

Listen to the following *words* and *useful expressions* and repeat. Then try to memorize them.

Words and Phrases

foggy	['fɔgi]	adj.	有雾的，多雾的
amazing	[ə'meiziŋ]	adj.	令人惊异的
reception	[ri'sepʃən]	n.	接待
due to			归因于
clear away			消散
kill the time			打发时间

Useful Expressions

1. The staff here told me that the flight had been delayed due to the foggy weather.
   机场人员告诉我因为大雾天气，航班延误了。
2. The weather report said that the fog will be cleared away in 2 hours.
   天气预报说大雾在 2 个小时内就会消散。

3. I'm afraid so.
   恐怕是的。
4. Why don't we kill the time by looking around the shops and stores here?
   我们可以在这里的商铺看看借以打发时间。
5. May be you will find something amazing!
   也许你能发现一些很不错的东西!
6. And it offers a large variety of antiques including: coins, pottery and traditional Chinese paintings.
   里面有各种古董包括钱币、瓷器及传统中国画。

Task 3

Dialogue I

Listen to the *dialogue I* for the first time. Then practice the dialogue by reading it aloud with your partner. Read through it at least twice, changing your role each time.

A Delayed Flight

【Scene】 *In the airport lobby, Zhang Hua, a young tour guide from the China Travel Service, is explaining to John smith about the delayed flight that he will take.*

　　　　J: John smith　　　　Z: Zhang Hua

J: Excuse me; did flight number FU88024 arrive in? I have been waiting here for an hour. And it should be arrived at half an hour ago. What's happened?

Z: I don't know, but Iwill ask the reception desk for it.(several minutes later)

Z: **The staff here told me that the flight had been delayed due to the foggy weather.**

J: Oh, it's terrible. Did they say when exactly will the flight arrive in?

Z: **The weather report said that the fog will be cleared away in 2 hours.**

J: That's to say we have to wait for another 90 minutes?

Z: **I'm afraid so.**

J: It's quite a long time to be here waiting the flight.

Z: **Why don't we kill the time by looking around the shops and stores here? May be you will find something amazing!**

J: That's a good idea! Is there any antique shop around here?

Z: Yes, it just around the corner over there. **And it offers a large variety**

Handling Customer Complaints   Item 14

of antiques including: **coins, pottery and traditional Chinese paintings.** What do you want to buy?
J: I just want to have a look around there.
Z: Ok, let's go!

Task 4

Listen and Answer

You will hear five questions. Listen carefully and give an appropriate answer to each of them.
(1) _____
(2) _____
(3) _____
(4) _____
(5) _____

Task 5

Role-play

Act out the following dialogs.

【Situation A】 Mr. Black, a tourist, is now complaining about the delayed flight to the tour guide at the airport.

Mr. Black:
☆ Complains to the tour guide.
☆ Asks about the arriving time.
☆ Shows anxiety.
☆ Asks if there are some other thing can do.
☆ Suggests to go to visit the nearest souvenir shop.

Tour guide:
☆ Promises to ask for the reason.
☆ Gives the reason why it's delayed.
☆ Gives the possible time when the flight will come.
☆ Suggests to look around for killing the time.
☆ Shows the nearest souvenir shop to Mr. Black.

【Situation B】 At the bus station, a foreign business traveler is complaining about the delayed bus to the tour guide.

Model 2
Complaining about the food   食品投诉

Task 1

Warm-up

Work in pairs. Try to answer the question below.

What kind of food do you like (or don't like)? Why?

Task 2

Learning Points

Listen to the following *words* and *useful expressions* and repeat. Then try to memorize them.

Words and Phrases

lamb	[læm]	n.	羔羊
inedible	[inedible]	adj.	不能吃的
fatty	['fæti]	adj.	油腻的
oily	['ɔili]	adj.	油腻的
recommendation	[ˌrekəmen'deiʃən]	n.	推荐
order	['ɔːdə]	v.	点菜
discount	[diskaunt]	n.	折扣
roast duck			烤鸭

Useful Expressions

1. What's up?
   发生了什么？
2. I will call the waiter to deal with it.
   我会叫服务生来处理的。
3. I've told them to make a change for you.
   我已经让他们给你重做一份。

Handling Customer Complaints　　Item 14

4. They promised to serve you in less than 5 minutes.
   他们许诺在 5 分钟内上菜。
5. They give us a 15% discount.
   他们给我们打了八五折。

Task 3

Dialogue II

Listen to the *dialogue II* for the first time. Then practice the dialogue by reading it aloud with your partner. Read through it at least twice, changing your role each time.

Complaining about the food

【Scene】 *A foreign tourist is complaining to the guide in a restaurant about the food.*
　　　　　　　　A: *the foreign tourist*　　　B: *the guide*

A:　Look, the food in this restaurant is so terrible!
B:　**What's up?**
A:　I hate to say, but this leg of lamb is inedible. It is so fatty. And the roast duck is too oily. In fact, it's the worst I've ever eaten!
B:　Mm. It did like what you say. **I will call the waiter to deal with it.**
　　(*Several minutes later*)
B:　Ok, **I've told them to make a change for you.**
A:　Will I wait for a long time?
B:　No need, **they promised to serve you in less than 5 minutes.**
A:　I also want to order a soup, What's your recommendation?
B:　I heard that the egg and vegetable soup here is quite delicious.
A:　Really? That's good. Could you please order one for me?
B:　No problem! (after meal)
A:　Can we make a discount for this?
B:　Of course, **they give us a 15% discount.**
A:　You are so nice!
B:　You are welcome.

Task 4

Listen and Answer

You will hear five questions. Listen carefully and give an appropriate answer to each of them.

(1) _____
(2) _____

(3) _____
(4) _____
(5) _____

Task 5

Role-play

Act out the following dialogs.

【Situation A】 You are escorting Mr. Black to have dinner in a restaurant. Mr. Black isn't satisfied with the food. You are asked to help Mr. Black to solve the problem.

Mr. Black:
- ☆ Complains about the food.
- ☆ Gives vivid descriptions.
- ☆ Asks for the serving time.
- ☆ Asks for discount.
- ☆ Gives thanks to the guide.

You:
- ☆ Asks for what happened.
- ☆ Promises that you will help Mr. Black to solve it.
- ☆ Says that the problem has solved.
- ☆ Tells the serving time.
- ☆ Tells the percentage of discount.

【Situation B】 At the restaurant, a foreign business traveler is complaining about the bad service and asking for your help.

Model 3
A Tour Guide or a Shopping Guide   导游还是导购

Task 1

Warm-up

Work in pairs. If you are a guide, when you are guiding your guests at a shop, what will you say to them? Discuss with your partner.

Handling Customer Complaints   Item 14

Task 2

Learning Points

Listen to the following *words* and *useful expressions* and repeat. Then try to memorize them.

Words and Phrases

unbelievable	[ˌʌnbɪˈliːvəbl]	adj.	难以置信的
kickback	[ˈkɪkbæk]	n.	佣金,回扣
scenic	[ˈsiːnɪk;ˈsenɪk]	n.	景色优美的
spot	[spɒt]	n.	地点，现场
terrible	[ˈterəbl]	adj.	糟糕的
responsibility	[rɪsˌpɒnsəˈbɪləti]	n.	责任
play an important role			扮演重要角色
hold belief			持有信念

Useful Expressions

1. There are some indeed, but not all.
   确实有一些，但不是全部。
2. The other important reason may be that by showing tourists around the stores a lot, the guide can kill a lot of time and save a large a amount of energy rather than by guiding them in a scenic spot.
   另一个重要的原因是带领游客逛商店会消磨很多时间并节省导游大量的精力。
3. It killed a lot of time and money of the tourists.
   这浪费了游客很多的时间和金钱。
4. But not all the guides act like this.
   但不是所有的导游都这样。
5. I always believe that it is our tour guide's responsibility to show beautiful sceneries as well as warm and kind service to our guests.
   我一直认为导游的职责是向游客展示美丽的风景和提供热情友好的服务。

Task 3

Dialogue III

Listen to the *dialogue III* for the first time. Then practise the dialogue by reading it aloud with your partner. Read through it at least twice, changing your role each time.

A Tour Guide or a Shopping Guide

【Scene】 *A tourist is discussing with a tour escort about whether today's guide is a tour guide or a shopping guide.*

　　　　　　　　A:　the tourist　　B:　the tour escort

A:　It's unbelievable that today's tour guide prefers to guide their tourists to stores than to scenic spots.

B:　**There are some indeed, but not all.**

A:　What do you think may lead to this situation?

B:　The kickback of course.

A:　Yeah. Money always plays an important role in it. But do you think there is any other reason?

B:　In my opinion, **the other important reason may be that by showing tourists around the stores a lot, the guide can kill a lot of time and save a large amount of energy rather than by guiding them in a scenic spot.**

A:　I couldn't agree with you more! But don't you think that's really hurt the tourists?

B:　Yes, **it killed a lot of time and money of the tourists.**

A:　How terrible!

B:　**But not all the guides act like this.** Actually, most of us did a good job in a trip. **I always believe that it is our tour guide's responsibility to show beautiful sceneries as well as warm and kind service to our guests.**

A:　You are right. And I hope every guide can hold the same belief like you!

B:　Thank you.

Task 4

Listen and Answer

You will hear five questions. Listen carefully and give an appropriate answer to each of them.

(1) _____

(2) _____

(3) _____

(4) _____

(5) _____

Handling Customer Complaints Item 14

Task 5

Role-play

Act out the following dialogs.

【Situation A】 You are an English tour guide who is explaining to a tourist about the responsibility of a tour guide.

Tourist:
- ☆ Gives impression of today's tour guide.
- ☆ Shows confusion of the responsibility.
- ☆ Asks for the reason.
- ☆ Shows his attitude (agree or disagree).
- ☆ Gives his own wish.

Guide:
- ☆ Makes a comment on the tourist's idea.
- ☆ Gives explanations.
- ☆ Shows your own attitude.
- ☆ Shows thanks.

【Situation B】 At a store, you are answering a tourist's question about shopping guide.

Model 4
A Complaint Letter on Holiday Booking　旅游度假投诉信

Task 1

Learning Points

Listen to the following *words* and *useful expressions* and repeat. Then try to memorize them.

Words and Phrases

arrangement	[əˈreindʒmənt]	*n.*	安排
balcony	[ˈbælkəni]	*n.*	阳台
faculty	[ˈfækəlti]	*n.*	职员
extra	[ˈekstrə]	*adj.*	额外的

exhaust	[ig'zɔːst]	v.	筋疲力尽
prompt	[prɔmpt]	adj.	迅速的
settle	[setl]	v.	解决
properly	['prɔpəli]	adv.	适当地
favorable	['feiərəbl]	adj.	满意的
favorable reply			满意的答复

Useful Expressions

1. I am writing to make a complaint about your poor arrangement of my booking which puts me in a very difficult position.
   去信告之你们对于我的预订的糟糕安排给我造成的困难局面。
2. But when I arrived at your hotel 5days ago, your faculty told me there is no vacancy any more.
   但当我5天前抵达你们酒店时，你们的员工告诉我没有空房间了。
3. Because your faculty causes the problems, I expect you to work with me to get a satisfactory resolution.
   因为是你的员工造成了这个问题，所以我希望你能够给我一个满意的解决办法。
4. I sincerely hope that you will give prompt attention to my case and settle it properly as soon as possible.
   我诚挚的希望此信能引起您足够的重视并能尽快加以解决。

Task 2

Passage Reading

Listen to the short passage for the first time. Then practice it by reading them aloud by yourself.

A Complaint Letter on Holiday Booking

Dear sir or madam,

  I am writing to make a complaint about your poor arrangement of my booking which puts me in a very difficult position.
  I booked a single room with a balcony face to the beach about 15 days ago. And the receiver promised me one. **But when I arrived at your hotel 5 days ago, your faculty told me there is no vacancy any more.** It's unbelievable! And then I had to spend extra money to find another hotel to live in with in the next 2 days, which make me feel exhausted and angry. **Because your faculty causes the problems, I expect you to work with me to get a satisfactory resolution:** to give back to me the money for the tow

Handling Customer Complaints Item 14

nights I spent at the other hotel.

I sincerely hope that you will give prompt attention to my case and settle it properly as soon as possible. I am looking forward to your favorable reply.

Sincerely,
Peterson

Task 3

Listen and Answer

You will hear five questions. Listen carefully and give an appropriate answer to each of them.

(1) _____
(2) _____
(3) _____
(4) _____
(5) _____

Task 4

Oral Practice

Retell the text in your own words.

Task 5

More Oral and Listening Practice:
【Listening】 Listen to the dialogs and fill in the blanks.

Listening I

Complaining about the Facilities in the Hotel Room

A: _____!
B: What's happened?
A: The facilities in my room are so poor! That the air-conditioning broke when I just turn it on.
B: In that case, _____.
A: Look, that's the _____ problem! I have asked the maintenance department _____ times, but no one answered my phone.

B: _____! They should at their place for_____.
   What's happen?
A: At last I called the _____. And they told me that all their repairmen are busy now.
B: What?! All of them?
A: Yes, _____.
B: What's wrong with them?_____.
A: Ok, thank you.
B: You are welcome.

Listening II

The Lost Luggage

A: What's happen to our _____? I haven't got it yet.
B: It should be arrived _____ before. Something must happened.
A: I just want to take a _____. I'm so tired. But now, what can I do?
B: Don't worry, I will ask the _____ to see what had happened.
A: It's totally _____. I have never ever meet with such kind of situation before.
B: I'm sure your luggage will _____. Wait for me.
A: So, what's the problem?
B: The manager said that it is the _____ which delayed the arrival of the luggage. They are now _____ to take them back here.
A: _____?
B: In no more than 40 minutes. You know it's rush hour now.

【Topics】 Divide the class into groups. Choose one of the following topics to discuss in each group. Give a short report about the group's opinion after that.

1. What is a tour guide's role in contact with the tourist's complaint?
2. What you should do to avoid too much complaints?
3. In order to build Beijing into a modern international city, many courtyards and hutongs in Beijing have been destroyed. Comment on this.

Item 15 Checking Out

结账退房服务

Model 1:
　　Paying the Hotel Bill in Cash   现金付账

Model 2:
　　Paying with Credit Card   信用卡付账

Model 3:
　　Paying with a Traveler's Check   支票付账

Model 4:
　　Checkout Service Procedures   退房结账程序

Model 1
Paying the Hotel Bill in Cash 现金付账

Task 1

Warm-up

Work in pairs. Learn the following words about checking out at the hotel and answer the question below.

| return the room key | clear the bills | settle the bills |

What should you do if you want to check out?

Task 2

Learning Points

Listen to the following *words* and *useful expressions* and repeat. Then try to memorize them.

Words and Phrases

bill	[bil]	n.	账单
receipt	[ri'si:t]	n.	收据
invoice	['invɔis]	n.	发票
change	[tʃeindʒ]	n.	零钱
service charge			服务费
advance deposit			预付金
in cash			用现金
check in			登记入住

Useful Expressions

1. I'd like to tell you that the checkout time is 12:00 noon.
   我想要告诉您退房时间是中午12点。

2. Can I get your name and room number, please?
   我能知道您的姓名和房间号码吗?
3. I'll print the bill for you.
   我将为您打印账单。
4. Sorry to have kept you waiting.
   抱歉让您等候。
5. Please check it.
   请核对。
6. You have paid an advance deposit of RMB 2,500, haven't you?
   你已经预付2500元押金，对吗?

Task 3

Dialogue I

Listen to the *dialogue I* for the first time. Then practise the dialogue by reading it aloud with your partner. Read through it at least twice, changing your role each time.

Paying the Hotel Bill in Cash

【Scene】*A guest wishes to pay his hotel bill in cash.*

S: Staff   G: Guest

S: Good morning, sir. May I help you?
G: We are leaving today, and I'd like to pay my bill now.
S: Certainly, sir. Oh, by the way, **I'd like to tell you that the checkout time is 12:00 noon. Can I get your name and room number, please?**
G: John Walker. Room 5006.
S: Yes, Mr. John Walker. You checked in three days ago on the afternoon of June 19, didn't you?
G: Yes.
S: And when are you leaving?
G: Right after lunch.
S: So you'll check out before 12:00?
G: Yes, exactly.
S: Just a moment, please. **I'll print the bill for you. Sorry to have kept you waiting.** Here you are. This is your bill, RMB 1,980, including 10 percent service charge. **Please check it.**
G: OK. Oh, that's right.

S: **You have paid an advance deposit of RMB 2,500, haven't you?**
G: Yes, here is the receipt.
S: Thank you. This is your invoice and your change, RMB 520. Count it, please.
G: That's quite all right. Goodbye.
S: We hope you'll enjoy your trip, Mr. Walker. Goodbye.

Task 4

Listen and Answer

You will hear five questions. Listen carefully and give an appropriate answer to each of them.

(1) _____
(2) _____
(3) _____
(4) _____
(5) _____

Task 5

Role-play

Act out the following dialogs.

【Situation A】 The guest is at the Front Desk and the receptionist receives him. The guest wants to check out.

The receptionist:
☆ Greets the guest.
☆ Asks the guest's name and room number.
☆ Asks if the guest has used any other service.
☆ Lets the guest wait.
☆ Prepares the guest's bill and tells the guest the total number.
☆ Tells that the guest has paid a deposit.
☆ Gives the guest his change and invoice.
☆ Hopes that the guests will have a good journey.

The guest:
☆ Greets the receptionist.
☆ Wants to settle the bill.
☆ Tells his name and room number.

Checking Out　　Item 15

- ☆ Says that there is no other service used.
- ☆ Checks the bill.
- ☆ Gives the receptionist the receipt of the deposit.
- ☆ Checks the change.
- ☆ Says goodbye to the receptionist.

【Situation B】 Mr. Clarke checks out at the Cashier's. The clerk asks the guest to exchange his US dollars into RMB.

Model 2
Paying with Credit Card　信用卡付账

Task 1

Warm-up

Work in pairs. Learn the following words about settling the bill at the hotel. Then answer the questions below.

| credit card | cash | traveler's check |

1. How many ways could you settle the bills?
2. Have you had such experience of using credit cards to buy something before? What does the receptionist/cashier do with your credit card?

Task 2

Learning Points

Listen to the following *words* and *useful expressions* and repeat. Then try to memorize them.

Words and Phrases

cash	[kæʃ]	n.	金
service	['sə:vis]	n.	务
folio	['fəuliəu]	n.	用户个人账目

imprint	[im'print]	n.	印
sign	[sain]	v.	签
credit card			信用卡
the Front Desk			前台

Useful Expressions

1. I'd like to check out, please.
   我想要结账。
2. Your bill totals…
   您的账单总计是……
3. Can I pay by my credit card?
   我能用信用卡付账吗?
4. Let me take an imprint of it.
   让我帮您压个印。
5. Please sign your name on the print.
   请把您的名字签在打印单上。

Task 3

Dialogue II

Listen to the *dialogue II* for the first time. Then practise the dialogue by reading it aloud with your partner. Read through it at least twice, changing your role each time.

Paying with Credit Card

【Scene】 *A guest comes to the Front Desk to check out by credit card.*

S: Staff   G: Guest

S: Good morning, sir. Can I help you?
G: **I'd like to check out, please.**
S: May I know your name and room number, sir?
G: I'm Mr. John Rich, Room 1508.
S: Yes. Have you used any other hotel services this morning?
G: No, I haven't used any services and I paid cash for my breakfast.
S: Fine. One moment while I check the folio. Three nights at RMB 500 each, and **your bill totals** RMB 1,500. Here you are. Have a check, please.

Checking Out   Item 15

G: Correct. But I don't have enough cash for it. **Can I pay by my credit card?**
S: Certainly, we do accept some major credit cards. What card do you have?
G: Visa Card.
S: Fine. **Let me take an imprint of it.**
G: Here it is.
S: Thanks. Just wait a moment. **Please sign your name on the print,** Mr. Rich.
G: OK. Here you are.
S: Thank you. Please take your credit card and keep the receipt.

Task 3

Listen and Answer

You will hear five questions. Listen carefully and give an appropriate answer to each of them.

(1) _____
(2) _____
(3) _____
(4) _____
(5) _____

Task 5

Role-play

Act out the following dialogs.

【Situation A】 The guest is at the Front Desk and the receptionist receives him. The guest wants to check out.

The receptionist:
☆ Greets the guest.
☆ Asks the guest's name and room number.
☆ Asks if the guest has used any facilities.
☆ Prepares the guest's bill.
☆ Tells the guest the total number.
☆ Asks how the guest likes to settle the bill.
☆ Takes an imprint of the card.

- ☆ Signs the guest's name on the print.
- ☆ Returns the credit card.
- ☆ Tells the guest to keep the receipt.

The guest:
- ☆ Greets the receptionist.
- ☆ Wants to settle the bill.
- ☆ Tells his name and room number.
- ☆ Answers that he has paid other services in cash.
- ☆ Checks the bill.
- ☆ Tells that he would like to use the credit card.
- ☆ Gives the receptionist the card.
- ☆ Says goodbye to the receptionist.

【Situation B】 At the Front Desk, the guest wants to check out by credit card and the clerk receives him.

Model 3
Paying with a Traveler's Check 支票付账

Task 1

Warm-up

Work in pairs. Think about the following question and discuss with your partner.

What are the differences between paying by credit card, in cash and with a traveler's check?

Task 2

Learning Points

Listen to the following *words* and *useful expressions* and repeat. Then try to memorize them.

Words and Phrases

charge	[tʃɑːdʒ]	v.	要价,支付费用
rate	[reit]	n.	费用,价格

Checking Out　　Item 15

| laundry | ['lɔːndri] | n. | 洗衣物 |
| passport | ['pɑːspɔːt] | n. | 护照 |

traveler's check　　　　　　　　　　旅行支票
room service　　　　　　　　　　　房内用膳服务
exchange rate　　　　　　　　　　 外汇牌价
exchange memo　　　　　　　　　　（外汇兑换）水单

Useful Expressions

1. Were you in Room 2816?
   您住 2816 房间？
2. One moment, please, and I'll get the bill ready.
   请稍等，我把您的账单准备好。
3. Please have a check.
   请您核对。
4. How would you like to pay your bill?
   您怎样支付您的账单？
5. May I see your passport, please?
   我能看下您的护照吗？
6. We hope you'll come again. Have a nice trip.
   欢迎您再来。旅途愉快！

Task 3

Dialogue III

Listen to the *dialogue III* for the first time. Then practise the dialogue by reading it aloud with your partner. Read through it at least twice, changing your role each time.

Paying with a Traveler's Check

【Scene】*A guest pays his bill in his traveler's check.*

　　　　　　　　　　S: staff　　G: guest

S: Good morning. Can I help you, sir?
G: I'd like to check out. The name is Alan Dick.
S: Excuse me, **were you in Room 2816?**
G: That's right. May I see the bill?
S: **One moment, please, and I'll get the bill ready.** ... It totals RMB 5,020. Here you are. **Please have a check.**
G: OK. Does this include service and tax?

S: Yes, that's everything. We charge you for the rate of the room, room service, laundry and drinks. Is that all right, Mr. Dick?
G: Yes, I don't see there is any problem with it.
S: **How would you like to pay your bill?**
G: In my traveler's check, if that's OK.
S: That'll do nicely. Thank you.
G: Can you tell me the exchange rate of US dollars for traveler's checks?
S: It's RMB 720 against 100 US dollars. **May I see your passport, please?**
G: Here you are.
S: Please sign your name on the traveler's check and sign again on the memo.
G: OK.
S: Here is your invoice. And this is the exchange memo.
G: Thank you. Goodbye.
S: **We hope you'll come again,** Mr. Dick. **Have a nice trip.** Goodbye.

Task 4

Listen and Answer

You will hear five questions. Listen carefully and give an appropriate answer to each of them.

(1) _____
(2) _____
(3) _____
(4) _____
(5) _____

Task 5

Role-play

Act out the following dialogs.

【Situation A】 The guest is at the Front Desk and the receptionist receives him. The guest wants to check out.

The receptionist:
☆ Greets the guest.
☆ Asks the guest's name and room number.
☆ Asks if the guest has used any facilities.

Checking Out　　Item 15

☆ Prepares the guest's bill, tells the guest the total number and explains the bill.
☆ Asks how the guest likes to settle the bill.
☆ Tells the guest the exchange rate.
☆ Wants to see the guest's passport.
☆ Gives the guest the invoice and the exchange memo.
☆ Hopes that he will come again.

The guest:
☆ Greets the receptionist.
☆ Wants to settle the bill.
☆ Tells his name and room number.
☆ Answers that he has paid other services in cash.
☆ Checks the bill.
☆ Tells that he would like to use the traveler's check.
☆ Asks the exchange rate.
☆ Gives the receptionist the passport.
☆ Signs the name on the traveler's check and the exchange memo.
☆ Says goodbye to the receptionist.

【Situation B】 Mr. Brown checks out at the reception. When the room attendant checks the rooms, she finds two bath towels missing.

Model 4
Checkout Service Procedures　退房结账程序

Task 1

Learning Points

Listen to the following *words* and *useful expressions* and repeat. Then try to memorize them.

Words and Phrases

procedure	[prə'si:dʒə]	n.	程序
greet	[gri:t]	v.	欢迎
fee	[fi:]	n.	费用
account	[ə'kaunt]	n.	账目，账户

input	['input]	v.	输入
incur	[in'kə:]	v.	发生（费用）
inquire	[in'kwaiə]	v.	询问，问明
extend	[iks'tend]	v.	转达，表达
in accordance with			与……一致
registration form			登记表

Useful Expressions

1. Asks the guest to show the room card and key card.
   请客人出示房卡和钥匙卡。
2. Prints out the bill.
   打印账单。
3. Asks the guest to sign on the printed copy.
   请客人在打印单上签名。
4. Extends thanks to the guests for their stay and wishes for them to visit the hotel again next time.
   对客人光临住店表示感谢，期待再次光临。

Task 2

Passage Reading

Listen to the short passage for the first time. Then practise it by reading it aloud by yourself.

Checkout Service Procedures

A. Greets the guest kindly when the guest comes to check out. **Asks the guest to show the room card and key card.**

B. Checks whether the room number on the room card is in accordance with the room number of the registration form.

C. Examines whether the fees incurred recently have been entered in to an account.

D. Checks whether all the accounts have been input in the computer.

E. If there is no error after check, **prints out the bill, and asks the guest to sign on the printed copy.**

F. Inquires how the guest would pay, and whether he/she has special requirements. Checks out according to different ways of payment that the guest requires.

Checking Out Item 15

G. At the end of checkout, **extends thanks to the guests for their stay and wishes for them to visit the hotel again next time.**

Task 3

Listen and Answer

You will hear five questions. Listen carefully and give an appropriate answer to each of them.

(1) _____
(2) _____
(3) _____
(4) _____
(5) _____

Task 4

Oral Practice

Retell the text in your own words.

Task 5

More Oral and Listening Practice:
【Listening】 Listen to the following dialogs and fill in the blanks.

Listening I

Exchanging Money

Cashier: Good afternoon! Can I help you?
Guest: Yes, I need to _____.
Cashier: _____?
Guest: What is _____ for the Euro?
Cashier: It's 8,00 to the Euro at the moment.
Guest: Well, I would like to change 500 Euros this time.
Cashier: Good. _____?
Guest: Yes. Here you are.
Cashier: Thank you. 500 Euros will be 4,000 yuan. _____
_____ and _____.

Guest: I'll take care of it. ... Is that all right?
Cashier: Yes, here is _____ and _____. Keep this _____.
Guest: Thank you for your help. Goodbye.
Cashier: Goodbye, Mr. Clarke. _____.

Listening II

A Mistake on the Hotel Bill

Staff: Can I help _____, please?
Guest: I'd like to check out, please.
Staff: _____, please?
Guest: Room 1408.
Staff: One moment while I _____.
Guest: Hmm, I thought the rate was 480 per night.
Staff: Exactly, sir.
Guest: What's this _____ of RMB _____?
Staff: Oh, that's a 10 percent _____.
Guest: Oh, OK. And this shows that I have a 108 _____. But I didn't use it.
Staff: Oh, I'm terribly sorry. This must be a mistake. I'll _____ _____ right away. Do you want to put your charges on your AMEX card?
Guest: Yes. That's right.
Staff: _____, please.
Guest: Here you are.
Staff: OK. Here's your copy, Mr. Smith. _____ _____.

【Topics】 Divide the class into groups. Choose one of the following topics to discuss in each group. Give a short report about the group's opinion after that.

1. Do you think it is right to severely punish a passenger joking about having a bomb? Why?
2. Does the last impression help to enhance the image of the tour guide? What should we do in order to set up a good impression to guests?
3. The loess plateau is said to be the source of the sand storms affecting Beijing and many other cities in north China. Talk about the causes and make some suggestions about how to stop them.

Item 16 Farewell, China

再见，中国

Model 1:
　　See You Again Soon　再见

Model 2:
　　Seeing Guests off at the Airport　机场送客

Model 3:
　　A Farewell Speech　欢送词

Model 1
See You Again Soon 再见

Task 1

Warm-up

Work in pairs. Think about the following two topics and discuss with your partners.

1. Suppose you are an English tour guide now, how would you bid farewell to your guests? What would you say to them?
2. Do you think bidding farewell is of equal importance to the greetings? Why?

Task 2

Learning Points

Listen to the following *words* and *useful expressions* and repeat. Then try to memorize them.

Words and Phrases

coach	[kəutʃ]	n.	旅游大巴车
accompany	[əˈkʌmpəni]	v.	陪同
sincerely	[sinˈsiəli]	adv.	真诚地
unforgettable	[ˌʌnfəˈgetəbl]	adj.	难忘的或"令人难忘的"
comment	[ˈkɔment]	n.	评论
tour group			旅游团
more or less			或多或少
say goodbye (to)			向某人告别
all the way			全程
on behalf of…			代表……
sweet sorrow			喜忧参半
give sb. a big hand			喝彩

Farewell, China　　Item 16

Useful Expressions

1. Your current visit to Shanghai is drawing to a close.
   大家的这次上海之行即将结束。
2. It is a good banquet that does not end.
   天下没有不散的宴席。
3. I hope you have enjoyed all your stay.
   希望你们在这里过得愉快。
4. Bon voyage!
   一路平安！
5. Could you fill out this form of evaluation for me?
   您能帮我填写一下评估表吗？
6. I'd like to express our heartfelt gratitude to you for your efforts and excellent services.
   对于你们所付出的努力和所提供的优质服务，我们表示忠心的感谢。

Task 3

Dialogue I

Listen to the *dialogue I* for the first time. Then practise the dialogue by reading it aloud with your partner. Read through it at least twice, changing your role each time.

See You Again Soon

【Scene】 *It is August 15. The tour group getting on the coach is leaving for the airport in the morning.*

　　　　L: Liu Hua (tour guide)　　M: Michael Wong (tour leader)

L:　　Hello, Mr. Wong, ladies and gentlemen, **your current visit to Shanghai is drawing to a close.** I would like to say a few words before you leave. There is an old Chinese saying, **"It is a good banquet that does not end"**. I think you can more or less guess the meaning of it. I really hate to do this, but the time has come for us to say goodbye. It has been a wonderful experience for me to accompany you all the way. **I hope you have enjoyed all your stay.** If there's anything that you are not satisfied with me, please do tell me so that I can do better in the future. And here, I'd like to take this opportunity to thank you all for your understanding, cooperation and support. I hope to see you again in the future and to be your guide. I sincerely hope that you'll come to visit China again. **Bon voyage!**

G:　　hank you, Miss Liu. You did a great job. We all had a very wonderful time. Let's give Miss Liu a big hand. *(Applause and cheers)*

L: Thank you. Before you leave, **could you fill out this form of evaluation for me?** The comments and suggestions that you provide will be very valuable to help plan future tours. *(Liu Hua collects the forms.)*

M: Thank you very much, Miss Liu. On behalf of the whole group, **I'd like to express our heartfelt gratitude to you for your efforts and excellent services.** We certainly have had a wonderful time in the past 5 days and will always remember this unforgettable journey. I believe, there will be further cooperation between us.

L: I suppose we have to, parting is such sweet sorrow. Hope to meet you again. Have a pleasant trip!

M: Thank you!

Task 4

Listen and Answer

You will hear five questions. Listen carefully and give an appropriate answer to each of them.

(1) _____
(2) _____
(3) _____
(4) _____
(5) _____

Task 5

Role-play

Act out the following dialogs.

【Situation A】 A tour guide is bidding farewell to a tour group who is leaving for his country. Before the guests leave, there are a large number of matters a tour guide must attend to:

☆ Asks the bellman to collect together the baggage which needs checking.
☆ Checks the amount of the baggage and whether they are locked or damaged with the tour leader.
☆ Helps the tourists to check out, reminds them to take their own items including their travel certificates, and warns them to take care of their valuables.

Farewell, China   Item 16

- ☆ Asks the tourists to check whether there is something for the local guide to deal with for them after their departure.
- ☆ Stands beside the door of the coach, and assists the tourists to get on.
- ☆ Counts the number of the tourists again, and confirms that no tourists' items are forgotten, then asks the driver to start.

【Situation B】 British Tour is now on the way to the airport. The tour guide is now bidding a farewell to her guests. They all feel regretful at parting because they all had a memorial experience.

Model 2
Seeing Guests off at the Airport   机场送客

Task 1

Warm-up

Work in pairs. Learn the following words and answer the questions below.

reconfirm	air ticket	Information Office	departure time	air flight
check-in desk	in advance	boarding card/pass	luggage claim card	

What are the procedure for checking in at the airport?

Task 2

Learning Points

Listen to the following *words* and *useful expressions* and repeat. Then try to memorize them.

Words and Phrases

cart	[kʌːt]	n.	手推车
lobby	[ˈlɔbi]	n.	大厅
interpret	[inˈtəːprit]	v.	讲解
boarding pass			登机牌
luggage claim card			行李牌

security-check 安全检查
group visa 团队签证

Useful Expressions

1. Here we are at the airport.
   现在我们到达机场了。
2. Would you please wait for me for a few seconds?
   请等我几分钟好吗?
3. Take your time.
   慢慢来。
4. It's time for us to say goodbye to each other.
   是我们相互道别的时候了。
5. Thank you for all your kindness.
   感谢您的好心。
6. Hope to see you soon.
   希望能再次见到您。
7. A happy journey home.
   回家旅途愉快。

Task 3

Dialogue II

Listen to the *dialogue II* for the first time. Then practise the dialogue by reading it aloud with your partner. Read through it at least twice, changing your role each time.

Seeing Guests off at the Airport

【Scene】 *Now the tour group has got off the coach, and the guests arrive at the gate of the airport.*
         J: Janet Jin (tour guide)   D: Daniel Black (tour leader)

J: **Here we are at the airport.** I will get some carts to carry your baggage.
D: Let me go with you.

【Scene】 *They return with the carts and put the suitcases on carts and push them to the lobby of the airport ... Now, they are inside the Airport Departure Lounge now.*

J: **Would you please wait for me for a few seconds?** I am going to get the boarding passes and luggage claim cards for you!
D: OK, **take your time.**

【Scene】 *The tour guide comes back. ...Now, it's time for them to say goodbye to each other.*

Farewell, China   Item 16

J: Thank you for your waiting. Here are your tickets, boarding passes and luggage claim cards. Please check them.
D: Thank you very much.
J: Shall we go for the security-check now?
D: OK. Let's go.
J: Please get your plane ticket, group visa and boarding pass ready.
D: Thanks for your help.
J: It's my pleasure.
D: Well, Miss Jin, **it's time for us to say goodbye to each other.**
J: Yes, I suppose we must. I have enjoyed all these days you have spent with us, and I'll always remember them. **Thank you for all your kindness.**
D: I have enjoyed your interpreting. You have done a wonderful job. I hope you'll be my guide again next time I'm here.
J: I hope so, too.
D: Good-bye, Miss Jin. **Hope to see you soon.**
J: Good-bye. **A happy journey home,** and hope to see you again soon.

Task 4

Listen and Answer

You will hear five questions. Listen carefully and give an appropriate answer to each of them.
(1) _____
(2) _____
(3) _____
(4) _____
(5) _____

Task 5

Role-play

Act out the following dialogs.

【Situation A】 You are an English tour guide who is saying goodbye to an American tour group at the airport. Mr. David is the tourist.

Tour guide:
☆ Asks to gather the baggage.
☆ Helps check in.

☆ Reminds to put the passport, credit card and travelers check in the suitcase so as to go through the security check.
☆ Tells that the airport tax is included in the air ticket.
☆ Expresses great honor to serve Mr. Davidson.
☆ Hopes that Mr. Davidson enjoys his trip home.
☆ Welcomes him to China again.

Mr. Davidson:
☆ Thanks to accompany to the airport
☆ Asks about the airport tax.
☆ Thanks for all having been done for him.
☆ Appreciates every minute of his stay here.
☆ Wishes everything goes well.

【Situation B】 The tourists are checking in at the airport with the local guide. With his help, the tourists go through the formalities required. Then they bid farewell at the security check.

Model 3
A Farewell Speech 欢送词

Task 1

Learning Points

Listen to the following *words* and *useful expressions* and repeat. Then try to memorize them.

Words and Phrases

distinguished	[dis'tiŋgwiʃt]	adj.	令人尊敬的
witness	['witnis]	v.	见证
occur	[ə'kə:]	v.	发生
economy	[i(:)'kɔnəmi]	n.	经济
symbol	['simbəl]	n.	象征
fragrance	['freɪgrəns]	n.	香味
seashore	['si:ʃɔ:]	n.	海滨
handicraft	['hændikrɑ:ft]	n.	手工艺品
promote	[prə'məut]	v.	改善,提高,促进

strengthen	[ˈstreŋθən]	v.	增强，增进
Confucius	[kənˈfju:ʃiəs]	n.	孔子
build up			建立
mausoleums of emperors			帝王陵墓
Nanxiang Bun			南翔小笼包
send one's best regards to			把……的祝福带给……

Useful Expressions

1. How time flies!
   时光飞逝。
2. Your trip to China is drawing to a close.
   你们来华的行程即将结束。
3. We thank you for coming.
   我们感谢诸位的来访。
4. We would thank you again for your great patience, cooperation and understanding, which have made our job easier.
   我们要再次感谢各位给予的良好耐心、有力合作和充分理解，这些使得我们工作变得容易。
5. The tour couldn't have been that successful without your support.
   没有各位的支持，这次旅游不可能如此成功。
6. There is nothing more delightful than to meet friends afar.
   有朋自远方来，不亦乐乎
7. I would like to welcome you back.
   但愿在将来的某个时候，与大家再相会。

Task 2

Passage Reading

Listen to the short passage for the first time. Then practise it by reading it aloud by yourself.

A Farewell Speech

My distinguished guests:

  How time flies! After over fifteen days, **your trip to China is drawing to a close.** You will leave Ningbo for America tomorrow morning. At this moment, please allow me to take this opportunity to say something on behalf of our China International Travel Service.

  First of all, **we thank you for coming.** Though it is pity that you cannot stay in our country any longer, it is long enough for us to build up our friendship. During these fifteen days, you have witnessed the great changes that have occurred in China. You have visited some big cities, Beijing as the capital city, Shanghai as the engine of China's economy, Xi'an as the home of Chinese culture and Ningbo as the symbol of the charming seaport etc. You have visited the beautiful countryside to witness farm life, as well, and to smell flower fragrance and breathe fresh air in the natural scenic spots. You have touched mysterious but charming Chinese culture, such as Chinese handicrafts, Peking Opera, and ancient mausoleums of emperors, and tasted delicious food, such as Beijing Roast Duck and Nanxiang Bun. All this will certainly promote your understanding of the economic and social development of China, and strengthen further business and cultural cooperation between our two countries.

Next, **we would thank you again for your great patience, cooperation and understanding, which have made our job easier. The tour couldn't have been that successful without your support**.

Lastly, we do hope that this goodbye is just the beginning of our friendship. Confucius, the greatest teacher in Chinese history, said that **"there is nothing more delightful than to meet friends afar"**. I believe that our friendship will grow fast and **I would like to welcome you back**, sometime in the future. Upon your return to America, please send my best regards to your families, your relatives, your friends and your colleagues.

Thank you!

Task 3

Listen and Answer

You will hear five questions. Listen carefully and give an appropriate answer to each of them.

(1) _____
(2) _____
(3) _____
(4) _____
(5) _____

Task 4

Oral Practice

Make a "Farewell Speech" with your partner. You should mention all the key points.

Farewell, China   Item 16

Task 5

More Oral and Listening Practice:
【Listening】Listen to the dialogs and fill in the blanks.

Listening I

Check-in at the Train Station

A: _____?
B: Yes, let's go on board to avoid the last minute rush.
A: _____. OK. Let's move on to the ticket control.
B: Where is the ticket control for going to Hangzhou?
A: Over there, at Gate 3. _____ and wait to get the tickets punched.
B: To which platform are we going?
A: Platform 3. _____.
B: Thank you.
A: Here we are. Platform 3. The car is just ahead. Car 6. Please get on.
B: It's a nice car. My seat is there.
A: _____, on the rack or under the seat?
B: On the rack, please. Thank you.
A: Good. _____?
B: No, thank you. You have been a great help. Thank you, indeed.
A: It's my pleasure. The train starts in a few minutes. Now it's time for us to say goodbye. _____.
B: Goodbye, Mr. Guide. Thank you for your help.

Listening II

Seeing Guests off

G: guide   T: tourists

G: Is everything in order now?
T1: Yes. _____?
G: At eleven thirty. There is still half an hour to go. _____.
T2: Mr. Hu, during our trip in the past ten days, you've shown your concern for us in every respect. I really don't know how to express

my gratitude.

G: _____.

T1: Before I came here, I only had an understanding of China from books and papers, television and films. Now I've seen China with my own eyes.

G: _____.

T1: It's a pity we haven't got enough time for many other places.

G: _____. You're always welcome.

T1: Wonderful. I hope we'll keep in touch.

G: _____.

T2: Goodbye, Mr.Hu. Thank you very much.

G: _____!

【Topics】 Divide the class into groups. Choose one of the following topics to discuss in each group. Give a short report about the group's opinion after that.

1. Many Chinese people including many students have experienced refusal to their visa application. What do you think are the most common reasons?

2. What can you do to make sure that you have made your guests satisfied?

3. The Yellow River has become a river above ground in the lower reaches threatening to cause destruction. Do you have any suggestions as to the solution to the problem?

Appendix 1 Scenic Spots and Historical Sites in China

中国各地名胜古迹

Anhui Province 安徽省
Huangshan Mountain 黄山
Jiuhua Mountain 九华山
Memorial Temple of Bao Zheng 包公祠
Anhui Provincial Museum 安徽省博物馆
Pagoda in Changqing Temple 长庆寺塔
Langya Mountain 琅琊山
Qiyun Mountain Scenic Spot 齐云山景区
Quarry Scenic Spot 采石风景名胜区
Taiji Cave Scenic Spot 太极洞风景名胜区
Tianzhu Mountain Scenic Spot 天柱山风景名胜区
Xidi Village and Hongcun Village 西递和宏村

Beijing Municipality 北京市
The Palace Museum 故宫
The Beihai Park 北海
The Ruins of Yuanmingyuan Palace 圆明园遗址
The Summer Palace 颐和园
The Temple of Heaven 天坛
The Thirteen Imperial Mausoleums of the Ming Dynasty 十三陵
the Tian'anmen Square 天安门广场
The China Millennium Monument 中华世纪坛
Badaling Great Wall 八达岭长城

Chongqing Municipality 重庆市
Golden Buddha Mountain Scenic Spot 金佛山风景名胜区
Jinyun Mountain 缙云山
Qutang Gorge 瞿塘峡
Wu Gorge 巫峡
Xiling Gorge 西陵峡
Dazu Stone Sculpture 大足石刻

Fujian Province 福建省
Gulangyu Island 鼓浪屿
Wuyi Mountain Scenic Spot 武夷山风景名胜区
Jimei Scenic Spot 集美景区
Jin Lake 金湖
Kaiyuan Temple 开元寺
Qingyun Mountain Scenic Spot 青云山风景名胜区
Tailao Mountain Scenic Spot 太姥山风景名胜区

Tianzhu Mountain Forest Park 天竺山森林公园

Gansu Province 甘肃省
Five Springs Park 五泉公园
Gansu Provincial Museum 甘肃省博物馆
The Giant Buddha Temple at Zhangye 张掖大佛寺
The Grottoes of Bingling Temple 炳灵寺石窟
Kongtong Mountain 崆峒山
Mingsha Mountain-Crescent Spring 鸣沙山-月牙泉
Mogao Grottoes 莫高窟
Tulugou National Forest Park 土鲁沟国家森林公园
Yellow River Iron Bridge 黄河铁桥

Guangdong Province 广东省
Dinghu Mountain 鼎湖山
Danxia Mountain 丹霞山
Huanghuagang Cemetery of Seventy-two Martyrs 黄花岗七十二烈士陵园
Seven Star Rock 七星岩
Sites of Huangpu Military Academy 黄埔军校旧址
Splendid China Folk Culture Village 锦绣中华民俗文化村
Sun Yatsen Memorial Hall 中山纪念堂
China Folk Culture Village 中华民俗文化村

Guangxi Zhuang Autonomous Region 广西壮族自治区
Cliff of Thousand-Buddha 千佛岩
Li River 漓江
Elephant Trunk Hill 象鼻山
Yangshuo 阳朔

Silver Beach 银滩
Ludi Cave 芦笛岩
Seven Star Park 七星公园

Guizhou Province 贵州省
Hongfu Temple 弘福寺
Nanjiao Park 南郊公园
Fanjing Mountain 梵净山
Huangguoshu Waterfall Scenic Spot 黄果树瀑布风景名胜区
Nine Dragon Cave Scenic Spot 九龙洞风景名胜区
Qianling Park 黔灵公园
Sites of Zunyi Conference 遵义会议会址
Nine Cave Sky Scenic Spot 九洞天风景名胜区

Hainan Province 海南省
Ends of the Earth 天涯海角
Five-finger Mountain 五指山
Yalong Bay 亚龙湾
Tropical Seashore Scenic Zone of Sanya City 三亚热带海滨风景名胜区

Hebei Province 河北省
Zhaozhou Bridge 赵州桥
Mulan Hunting Ground 木兰围场
East Mausoleum of the Qing Dynasty 清东陵
West Mausoleum of the Qing Dynasty 清西陵
Chengde Mountain Resort 承德避暑山庄
Shanhai Pass 山海关
Beidaihe 北戴河
Guanghui Temple 广惠寺
Handan Old City of the Zhao State 赵邯郸故城
Meng Jiangnv's Temple 孟姜女庙

Xibaipo Village 西柏坡
Yansai Lake 燕塞湖

Henan Province 河南省
Longmen Grottoes 龙门石窟
Songshan Mountain 嵩山
White Horse Temple 白马寺
Songyang Academy 嵩阳书院
Henan Museum 河南博物馆
Shaolin Temple 少林寺
Yuhuang Pavilion of Yanqing Temple 延庆观玉皇阁
YellowRiver Scenic Zone 黄河风景区

Heilongjiang Province 黑龙江省
Wudalianchi Scenic Spot 五大连池风景名胜区
Jingpo Lake Scenic Spot 镜泊湖风景名胜区
Northeast Tiger Garden 东北虎林园
Double-dragon Scenic Spot 二龙山风景区
Sun Island 太阳岛
Yabuli Skiing Resort 亚布力滑雪场
Zhalong Nature Reserve 扎龙自然保护区

Hubei Province 湖北省
Huanghe Tower 黄鹤楼
Jingzhou Museum 荆州博物馆
Jiugong Mountain Scenic Spot 九宫山风景名胜区
Dahong Mountain Scenic Spot 大洪山风景名胜区
East Lake Scenic Spot 东湖风景区
Memorial Hall of Wuchang Uprising in 1911 Revolution 辛亥革命武昌起义纪念馆
Shennongjia 神农架
Wudang Mountain 武当山

Hunan Province 湖南省
Aiwan Pavilion 爱晚亭
Ancient Town of Fenghuang 凤凰古城
Yueyang Tower 岳阳楼
Heng Mountain 衡山
Shao Mountain 韶山
Wulingyuan Scenic and Historic Interest Area 武陵源风景区
Yuelu Academy 岳麓书院
Yuelu Mountain 岳麓山
Zhangjiajie National Forest Park 张家界国家森林公园

Jilin Province 吉林省
Century Square 世纪广场
Changbai Mountain 长白山
Maoer Mountain National Forest Park 帽尔山国家森林公园
Royal Palace of the Puppy Manchurian State 伪满洲国皇宫
Songhua Lake Scenic Spot 松花湖风景名胜区
Tianchi Lake of Changbai Mountain 长白山天池
Yalu River 鸭绿江

Jiangsu Province 江苏省
Lion Grove Garden 狮子林
Shouxi Lake 瘦西湖
Humble Administrator's Garden 拙政园
Tuisi Garden 退思园
Master-of-Net Garden 网师园
Lingering Garden 留园
Ancient Canal 古运河
Daming Temple 大明寺
Cold Mountain Temple 寒山寺

Huqiu Hillock 虎丘
Yuhua Terrace 雨花台
Dr.Sun Yet-san's Mausoleum 中山陵
Zhou Village 周庄
Mao Mountain 茅山
Nanjing Massacre Memorial Hall 南京大屠杀纪念馆
Nanjing Yangtze River Bridge 南京长江大桥
Qinhuai River 秦淮河
Shajiabang Town 沙家浜
Shugang Slim West Lake Scenic Spot 蜀岗瘦西湖风景名胜区
Tai Lake Scenic Spot 太湖风景名胜区
Wuxi Movie City 无锡影视城

Jiangxi Province 江西省
Jinggang Mountain 井冈山
Lu Mountain 庐山
Sanqing Mountain 三清山
August 1th Nanchang Uprising Museum 八一南昌起义纪念馆
Jingdezhen Porcelain Museum 景德镇陶瓷管
Meiling Mountain and Prince Teng's Pavilion Scenic Spot 梅岭滕王阁风景名胜区
Poyang Lake 鄱阳湖

Liaoning Province 辽宁省
Golden Stone Beach Scenic Spot 金石滩风景名胜区
Guomen Park 国门公园
Qian Mountain Scenic Spot in Anshan City 鞍山千山风景区
Imperial Palace in Shenyang 沈阳故宫
Star Sea Park 星海公园
Tiger Beach Park 老虎滩公园
Yalu River Scenic Spot 鸭绿江风景名胜区
Anti-America and Supporting-Korea War Memorial Hall 抗美援朝纪念馆
Dalian-Lvshunkou Beach Resort 大连—旅顺口海滨

Inner Mongolia Autonomous Region 内蒙古自治区
Genghis Khan's Mausoleum 成吉思汗陵
Grand Mosque 清真大寺
Dazhao Lamasery 大昭寺
Zhaojun's Tomb 昭君墓
Hulun Beier Meadow 呼伦贝尔草原
Singing Sand Slope 响沙湾

Ningxia Hui Autonomous Region 宁夏回族自治区
Imperial Mausoleums of the Western Xia Dynasty 西夏王陵
Sand Lake 沙湖
Cliff Carvings of Helan Mountain 贺兰山岩画

Qinghai Province 青海省
Great Temple of Golden Tile 大金瓦寺
Lesser Temple of Golden Tile 小金瓦寺
Qinghai Lake and Bird Island 青海湖和鸟岛
Mengdalin Nature Reserve 孟达林自然保护区
Ta'er Lamasery 塔尔寺

Shandong Province 山东省
Tai Mountain 泰山
Confucius' Temple 孔庙
Kong Family Mansion 孔府
Cemetery of Confucius 孔林
Thousand-Buddha Cliff 千佛岩

Thousand-Buddha Mountain 千佛山
Baotu Spring 趵突泉
Daming Lake 大明湖
Penglai Pavilion 蓬莱阁
Black Tiger Spring 黑虎泉
Yellow River Dikes 黄河河堤
Wooden Pagoda in Yingxian County 应县木塔

Shanxi Province 山西省
Heng Mountain 恒山
Hukou Waterfall of the Yellow River 黄河壶口瀑布
Yungang Grottoes 云冈石窟
Jin Ancestral Temple 晋祠
Pingyao Ancient City 平遥古城
Qiao's Mansion 乔家大院
Wutai Mountain 五台山
Yanmen Pass 雁门关

Shaanxi Province 陕西省
City Wall 古城墙
Huaqing Hot Spring 华清池
Hua Mountain Scenic Spot 华山风景名胜区
Hukou Waterfall 壶口瀑布
Li Mountain Scenic Spot 骊山风景名胜区
Mausoleum of the First Qin Emperor and Terracotta Warriors and Horses 秦始皇陵兵马俑
Yellow Emperor's Mausoleum 黄帝陵
Great Mosque 大清真寺
Big Wild Goose Pagoda 大雁塔
Small Wild Goose Pagoda 小雁塔

Shanghai Municipality 上海市
Jade Buddha Temple 玉佛寺
Chenghuang Temple 城隍庙
Oriental Pearl Tower 东方明珠塔
The Band 外滩
Yuyuan Garden 豫园
International Convention Center 国际会议中心
Jinmao Edifice 金茂大厦
Zhujiajiao Town 朱家角镇

Sichuan Province 四川省
Leshan Big Buddha 乐山大佛
E'mei Mountain 峨眉山
Huanglong Scenic Spot 黄龙风景区
Jiuzhai Valley Scenic Spot 九寨沟风景区
Dujiangyan Irrigation System 都江堰
Longmen Mountain Scenic Spot 龙门山风景名胜区
Qingcheng Mountain 青城山

Taiwan Province 台湾省
Alishan Scenic Area 阿里山风景区
Danshui Scenic Spot 淡水风景区
Sun and Moon Pools 日月潭
The Palace Museum 故宫博物院
Yangming Mountain 阳明山
Zheng Chenggong Temple 郑成功庙

Tianjin Municipality 天津市
Dagukou Emplacement 大沽口炮台
Eight Immertals'Table Reserve at Ji County 蓟县八仙桌子保护区
Guangdong Assembly Hall 广东会馆
Jingyuan Garden 静园
Tianhou Palace 天后宫
Tianjin Natural History Museum 天津自然历史博物馆
Yuhuang Pavilion 玉皇阁

Tibet Autonomous Region 西藏自治区
Potala Palace 布达拉宫

Jokhang Temple 大昭寺
Everest 珠穆朗玛峰
Norbu Lingka 罗布林卡
Yarlung Zangbo Grand Canyon 雅鲁藏布大峡谷

Xinjiang Uygur Autonomous Region 新疆维吾尔自治区
Tianchi Lake of Tianshan Mountian 天山天池
Kanas Lake 哈纳斯湖
Altun Mountain Nature Reserve 阿尔金山自然保护区
Bayin Bulud Swan Lake 巴音布鲁克天鹅湖
Flame Mountain 火焰山
Karez Well 坎儿井
Loulan Ancient City 楼兰古城
Grape Gully 葡萄沟

Yunnan Province 云南省
Cang Mountain 苍山
Dianchi Lake 滇池
Erhai Lake 洱海
Ethnic Town of Yunnan Province 云南民族村
Kunming World Horticulture Expo Park 昆明世界园艺博然会
Lijiang Ancient City 丽江古城
Stone Forest Scenic Spot 石林风景名胜区
Tiger Springing Gorge 虎跳峡
Jade Dragon Jokul 玉龙雪山
Dali 大理
Xishuangbanna 西双版纳

Zhejiang Province 浙江省
Putuo Mountain Scenic Spot 普陀山风景名胜区
Fuchun River-Xin'an River Scenic Spot 富春江—新安江景区
West Lake Scenic Spot 西湖风景名胜区
Jiufeng Mountain-Dafo Temple Scenic Zone 九峰山—大佛寺景区
Ancient Xitang Town 西塘古镇
Hemudu Sites 河姆渡遗址
Keyan Rock 柯岩
Longyou Grottoes 龙游石窟
South Lake in Jiaxing City 嘉兴南湖
Qiandao Lake 千岛湖
Tiantai Mountain Scenic Zone 天台山风景名胜区
Tianyi Pavilion 天一阁
Wu Town 乌镇
Xiandu Scenic Spot 仙都风景名胜区
Xuedou Mountain Scenic Spot 雪窦山风景名胜区
Yandang Mountain 雁荡山
Xikou-Home Town of Chiang Kai-shek 蒋介石故里溪口
Lingyin Temple 灵隐寺
Orchid Pavilion 兰亭
Temple and Tomb of Yu The Great 大禹陵
Lu Xun's Former Residence 鲁迅故居

Hong Kong Special Administrative Region 香港特别行政区
Wong Tai Sin Temple 黄大仙祠
Hong Kong Convention and Exhibition Center 香港会展中心
Ocean Park 海洋公园
Qingma Bridge 青马大桥
Victoria Park 维多利亚公园

Macao Special Administrative Region 澳门特别行政区
Mage Temple 妈阁庙
Big Barbette 大炮台
Dasanba Memorial Arch 大三巴牌坊

Appendix 2 Famous Chinese Historical and Cultural Cities

中国历史文化名城

Provinces	Cities and counties
Anhui Province	Shou County 寿县, She County 歙县, Bozhou 亳州, Jixi County 绩溪, Anqing 安庆
Fujian Province	Quanzhou 泉州, Fuzhou 福州, Zhangzhou 漳州, Changting 长汀
Gansu Province	Dunhuang 敦煌, Tianshui 天水, Zhangye 张掖, Wuwei 武威
Guangdong Province	Guangzhou 广州, Chaozhou 潮州, Zhaoqing 肇庆, Foshan 佛山, Meizhou 梅州, Leizhou 雷州
Guangxi Zhuang Autonomous Region	Guilin 桂林, Liuzhou 柳州
Guizhou Province	Zunyi 遵义, Zhenyuan 镇远
Hainan Province	Qiongshan 琼山, Haikou 海口
Hebei Province	Baoding 保定, Chengde 承德, Zhengding 正定, Handan 邯郸, Shanhaiguan (Qinhuangdao) 山海关区（秦皇岛）
Heilongjiang Province	Harbin 哈尔滨
Henan Province	Luoyang 洛阳, Anyang 安阳, Jun County 浚县, Nanyang 南阳, Puyang 濮阳, Shangqiu 商丘, Zhengzhou 郑州, Kaifeng 开封
Hubei Province	Wuhan 武汉, Jingzhou 荆州, Xiangfan 襄樊, Suizhou 随州, Zhongxiang 钟祥
Hunan Province	Changsha 长沙, Yueyang 岳阳, Fenghuang 凤凰
Inner Mongolia Autonomous Region	Hohhot 呼和浩特
Jiangsu Province	Nanjing 南京, Suzhou 苏州, Yangzhou 扬州, Xuzhou 徐州, Huai'an 淮安, Zhenjiang 镇江, Changzhou 常州, Wuxi 无锡
Jiangxi Province	Jingdezhen 景德镇, Nanchang 南昌, Ganzhou 赣州
Jilin Province	Jinlin 吉林, Ji'an 集安
Liaoning Province	Shenyang 沈阳
Ningxia Hui Autonomous Region	Yinchuan 银川
Qinghai Province	Tongren 同仁

(续表)

Provinces	Cities and counties
Shaanxi Province	Xi'an 西安, Yan'an 延安, Hancheng 韩城, Yulin 榆林, Xianyang 咸阳, Hanzhong 汉中
Shandong Province	Qufu 曲阜, Jinan 济南, Qingdao 青岛, Liaocheng 聊城, Zoucheng 邹城, Linzi 临淄, Taian 泰安
Shanxi Province	Datong 大同, Pingyao 平遥, Xinjiang 新绛, Dai County 代县, Qi County 祁县
Sichuan Province	Chengdu 成都, Langzhong 阆中, Leshan 乐山, Dujiangyan 都江堰, Luzhou 泸州, Zigong 自贡, Yibin 宜宾
Tibet Autonomous Region	Lhasa 拉萨, Xigaze 日喀则, Gyangze 江孜
Xinjiang Autonomous Region	Kashi 喀什, Tulufan 吐鲁番, Tekesi 特克斯
Yunnan Province	Kunming 昆明, Dali 大理, Lijiang 丽江, Jianshui 建水, Weishan 巍山
Zhejiang Province	Hangzhou 杭州, Shaoxing 绍兴, Ningbo 宁波, Quzhou 衢州, Linhai 临海, Jinhua 金华

Appendix 3 The National Key Attractions and Scenic Spots

国家重点风景名胜区

Anhui Province 安徽省
Mount Huangshan 黄山
Mount Jiuhua 九华山
Chao Lake 巢湖
Taiji Cave 太极洞
Mount Tianzhu 天柱山
Mount Langya 琅琊山
Mount Qiyun 齐云山
Caishi 采石
Huating Lake 花亭湖

Beijing Municipality 北京市
Badaling-Thirteen Tombs of the Ming Dynasty 八达岭—十三陵
Stone Flower Cave 石花洞

Chongqing Municipality 重庆市
Golden Buddha Mountian 金佛山
Mount Jinyun 缙云山
Simian Mountain 四面山
Lotus River 芙蓉江
Sky Crevice and Earth Canyon 天坑地缝
Three Gorges of the Yangtze Rive 长江三峡

Fujian Province 福建省
Mount Wuyi 武夷山
Mount Qingyuan 清源山
Gulangyu-Mount Wanshi 鼓浪屿—万石山
Mount TaiLao 太姥山
Taoyuan Caves-Linyin Stone Forest 桃花源—鳞隐石林
Yuanyang Creek 鸳鸯溪
Mount Guanzhi 冠豸山
Yuhua Cave 玉华洞
Mount Qingyun 青云山
Gold Lake 金湖

Gansu Province 甘肃省
Mount Maiji 麦积山
Mogao Caves 莫高窟
Mount Mingsha 鸣沙山
Crescent Spring 月牙泉

Guangdong Province 广东省
Mount Xiqiao 西樵山
Mount Luofu 罗浮山
Mount Danxia 丹霞山

Mount Baiyun 白云山
Huguang Rock Lake 湖光岩

Guangxi Zhuang Autonomous Region 广西壮族自治区
Li River in Guilin City 桂林漓江
West Mountain of Guiping City 桂平西山
Flower Mountain 花山

Guizhou Province 贵州省
Huangguoshu Falls 黄果树
Zhijin Cave 织金洞
Red Maple Lake 红枫湖
Dragon Palace 龙宫
Red River 赤水
Mount Doupeng of Dujun & Sword River 都匀斗篷山一剑江
Nine Cave Sky 九洞天
Nine-dragon Cave 九龙洞
Dong Village Scenic Spot in Liping County 黎平洞乡

Hainan Province 海南省
Tropical Seashore in Sanya City 三亚热带海滨

Hebei Province 河北省
Chengde Mountain Resort and Eight Outlying Temples 承德避暑山庄外八庙
Qinhuangdao 秦皇岛
Beidaihe 北戴河
Xibaipo Village 西柏坡
Mount Tiangui 天桂山

Heilongjiang Province 黑龙江省
Jingpo Lake 镜泊湖
Wudalianchi 五大连池

Henan Province 河南省
Longmen Grottoes 龙门石窟
Mount Song 嵩山
Mount Wangwu and Mount Yuntai 王屋山一云台山
Qingtian River 青天河
Mount Shennong 神农架

Hubei Province 湖北省
Mount Wudang 武当山
Mount Dahong 大洪山
Longzhong 隆中
Mount Jiugong 九宫山
Lushui River 陆水

Hunan Province 湖南省
Mount Heng 衡山
Wulingyuan 武陵源
Yueyang Tower 岳阳楼
Dongting Lake 洞庭湖
Shao Mountain 韶山
Yuelu Mountain 岳麓
Mount Lang 崀山
Taohuayuan 桃花源

Inner Mongolia Autonomous Region 内蒙古自治区
Zhalantun 扎兰屯

Jiangsu Province 江苏省
Lake Tai 太湖
Mount Zhong of Nanjing City 南京钟山
Shouxi Lake 瘦西湖
Mount Yuntai 云台山
Three Mountains 三山

Jiangxi Province 江西省
Mount Lu 庐山

Mount Jinggang 井冈山
Mount Dragon and Tiger 龙虎山
Fairy Lake 仙女湖
Peak Mei and Prince Teng's Pavilion 梅岭—滕王阁

Jilin Province 吉林省
Lake Songhua 松花湖
Xianjing Terrace 仙景台
Badabu and Jingyue Pool 八大部—净月潭

Liaoning Province 辽宁省
River Yalu 鸭绿江
Golden Stone Beach 金石滩
Mount Qian 千山
Dalian and Lvshunkou 大连—旅顺口
Benxi Water Cave 本溪水洞

Ningxia Hui Autonomous Region 宁夏回族自治区
Imperial Mausolems of the Western Xia Kingdom 宁夏西夏王陵

Qinghai Province 青海省
Qinghai Lake 青海湖

Shaanxi Province 陕西省
Mount Hua 华山
Mount Li 临潼骊山
Terracotta Warriors and Horses 兵马俑
Mount Tiantai in Baoji City 宝鸡天台山
Yellow Emperor's Mausoleum 黄帝陵
Qiachuan of Heyang County 合阳洽川

Shanxi Province 山西省
Mount Wutai 五台山
Mount Heng 恒山

North Wudang Mountain 北武当山
Hukou Falls of the Yellow River 黄河壶口瀑布
Mount Wulao 五老峰

Shandong Province 山东省
Mount Tai 泰山
Seaside of Jiaodong Peninsular 胶东半岛海滨
Qingzhou 青州

Sichuan Province 四川省
Mount Emei 峨眉山
Huanglong Temple 黄龙寺
Jiuzhai Valley 九寨沟
Dujiangyan 都江堰
Mount Qingcheng 青城山
Shu Road of Jianmen Pass 剑门蜀道
Xiling Jokul 西岭雪山
Mount Longmen 龙门山

Tianjin Municipality 天津市
Mount Pan 盘山

Tibet Autonomous Region 西藏自治区
Yalong River 雅砻江

Xinjiang Uygur Autonomous Region 新疆维吾尔自治区
Tianchi Lake of Tianshan Mountain 天山天池
Kumutage Desert 库木塔格沙漠
Lake Sailimu 赛里木湖

Yunnan Province 云南省
Stone Forest of Lunan 路南石林
Dali 大理
Xishuangbanna 西双版纳

Lake Dian of Kunming City 昆明滇池
Jade Dragon Jokul 玉龙雪山
Ruilijiang River 瑞丽江
Jianshui 建水
Alu 阿庐

Zhejiang Province 浙江省
West Lake of Hangzhou City 杭州西湖
Mount Putuo 普陀山
Fuchunjiang River 富春江

Xin'anjiang River 新安江
Lake of a Thousand Island 千岛湖
Mount Xuedou 雪窦山
Mount Yandang 雁荡山
Mount Tiantai 天台山
Duble-dragon 双龙
Xianju 仙居
Wuxie 五泄
Changyu Dongtian 长屿硐天

Appendix 4 A Brief Chinese Chronology

中国历史年代简表

Name of Dynasty 朝代			Period 年代	Seat of Capital 都城
Xia Dynasty 夏			C.2100—C.1600 B.C.	Yangcheng (E. Dengfeng, Henan) 阳城（河南登封东）
Shang Dynasty 商			C.1600—C.1100 B.C.	Bo (Shangqiu, Henan) 亳（河南商丘附近）
Zhou Dynasty 周	Western Zhou Dynasty 西周		C.1100—771 B.C.	Gaojing (W. Xi'an) 镐京（陕西西安西）
	Eastern Zhou Dynasty 东周 Spring and Autumn Period 春秋 Warring States 战国		770—256 B.C. 770—476 B.C. 475—221 B.C.	Luoyi (Luoyang, Henan) 洛邑（河南洛阳）
Qin Dynasty 秦			221—206 B.C.	Xianyang (Shaanxi) 咸阳（陕西）
Han Dynasty 汉	Western Han 西汉		206 B.C.—24 A.D.	Chang'an (Xi'an, Shaanxi) 长安（西安）
	Eastern Han 东汉		25—220 A.D.	Luoyang (Henan) 洛阳（河南）
Three Kingdoms 三国	Wei 魏		220—265	Luoyang (Henan) 洛阳（河南）
	Shu Han 蜀汉		221—263	Chengdu (Sichuan) 成都（四川）
	Wu 吴		222—280	Jianye (Nanjing, Jiangsu) 建业（今江苏南京）
Western Jin Dynasty 西晋			265—316	Luoyang (Henan) 洛阳（河南）
Eastern Jin Dynasty 东晋			317—420	Jiankang (nanjing) 建康（今南京）
Northern and Southern Dynasties 南北朝	Southern Dynasties 南朝	Song 宋	420—479	Jiankang (nanjing) 建康（今南京）
		Qi 齐	479—502	Jiankang (nanjing) 建康（今南京）
		Liang 梁	502—557	Jiankang (nanjing) 建康（今南京）
		Chen 陈	557—589	Jiankang (nanjing) 建康（今南京）
	Northern Dynasties 北朝	Northern Wei 北魏	386—534	Pingcheng (Datong, Shanxi) 平城（山西大同）
		Eastern Wei 东魏	534—550	Ye (Southwest Linzhang, Hebei) 邺（河北临漳西南）
		Northern Qi 北齐	550—557	Ye (Southwest Linzhang, Hebei) 邺（河北临漳西南）
		Western Wei 西魏	535—556	Chang'an (Xi'an) 长安（今西安）
		Northern Zhou 北周	557—581	Chang'an (Xi'an) 长安（今西安）

(续表)

Name of Dynasty 朝代			Period 年代	Seat of Capital 都城
Sui Dynasty 隋			581—618	Daxing (Xi'an) 大兴（今西安）
Tang Dynasty 唐			618—907	Chang'an (Xi'an) 长安（今西安）
Five Dynasties & Ten Kingdoms 五代十国	Five Dynasties 五代	Later Liang 后梁	907—923	Bian (Kaifeng) 汴 （今河南开封）
		Later Tang 后唐	923—936	Luoyang, Henan 河南洛阳
		Later Jin 后晋	936—946	Bian (Kaifeng) 汴 （今河南开封）
		Later Han 后汉	947—950	Bian (Kaifeng) 汴 （今河南开封）
		Later Zhou 后周	951—960	Bian (Kaifeng) 汴 （今河南开封）
	Ten Kingdoms 十国	Wu 吴	902—937	Yangzhou, Jiangsu 江苏扬州
		Southern Tang 南唐	937—975	Jinling (Nanjing) 金陵（今江苏南京）
		Wu Yue 吴越	907—978	Hangzhou, Zhejiang 浙江杭州
		Chu 楚	907—951	Changsha, Hunan 湖南长沙
		Min 闽	909—945	Changle (Fuzhou, Fujian) 长乐（今福建福州）
		Southern Han 南汉	917—971	Guangzhou, Guangdong 广东广州
		Former Shu 前蜀	903—925	Chengdu, Sichuan 四川成都
		Later Shu 后蜀	933—965	Chengdu, Sichuan 四川成都
		Jingnan 荆南	924—963	Jingzhou, Hubei 荆州（今湖北）
		Northern Han 北汉	951—979	Taiyuan (Shanxi) 太原（山西）
Song Dynasty 宋	Northern Song Dynasty 北宋		960—1127	Kaifeng (Henan) 开封（河南）
	Southern Song Dynasty 南宋		1127—1279	Lin'an (Hangzhou) 临安（今杭州）
Liao Dynasty 辽			916—1125	Huangdu (Bairin Zuoqi, Inner Mongolia) 黄都 （今内蒙巴林左旗）
Western Xia 西夏			1038—1227	Xingqingfu, (Yinchuan, Ningxia) 兴庆府（今宁夏银川）
Jin Dynasty 金			1115—1234	Zhongdu (now Beijing) 中都（今北京）
Yuan Dynasty 元			1279—1368	Dadu (now Beijing) 大都（今北京）
Ming Dynasty 明			1368—1644	Yingtianfu 应天府 （Nanjing）、Beijing
Qing Dynasty 清			1644—1911	Beijing 北京
Republic of China "中华民国"			1912—1949	Nanjing 南京
People's Republic of China 中华人民共和国			Founded in 1949	Beijing 北京

Appendix 5 The Ten Different Cooking Styles in China

中国十大菜系

Sichuan Style 四川菜
Pork shreds with fishy flavour 鱼香肉丝
Bean curd with mince and chilli oil 麻婆豆腐
Diced chicken with chilli pepper 宫保鸡丁
Stewed scallop and turnip ball 绣球干贝
Steamed pork wrapped in lotus leaves 荷叶蒸肉
Translucent beef slices 灯影牛肉
Spicy Sichuan-style tender chicken slices 怪味鸡块
Shrimp with green vegetables 翡翠虾仁

Shandong Style 山东菜
Dezhou grilled chicken 德州扒鸡
Chinese yam in hot toffee 拔丝山药
Quick-boiled clam 油爆大蛤
Lotus flower and shrimp 荷花大虾
Bird's nest in clear soup 清汤燕窝
Braised sea whelks in brown sauce 红烧海螺
Braised sea slug with crab meat in brown sauce 蟹烧海参

Guangdong Style 广东菜
Stewed crab meat and eggplant 虾肉烧茄子
Stuffed duck shaped as gourd 八珍葫芦鸭
Crisp-skinned chicken 脆皮鸡
Sliced chicken with oyster sauce 蚝油滑鸡片
Roasted suckling pig 烤乳猪
Shark's fin with crab ovum 虾黄鱼翅
Sweet-sour pork fillet with chilli 糖醋咕噜肉

Jiangsu Style or Huaiyang Style 江苏菜（淮扬菜）
Chicken mousse broth with fresh corn 鸡茸玉米
Yincai vegetables cooked with chicken slices 银菜鸡丝
Scallop wrapped in chicken breast slices 鸡片包干贝
Squid with crispy rice crust 鱿鱼锅巴
Crab meat & minced pork ball in casserole 蟹粉狮子头

Fujian Cuisine 福建（闽）菜

Sea food and poultry in casserole 佛跳墙
Steamed chicken ball with egg-white 蒸芙蓉鸡球
Fried prawn shaped as a pair of fish 太极明虾
Saute shredded whelks in rice wine sauce 炝糟响螺
Steamed pork roll with rice flour and lotus leaf 荷叶米粉肉
Crisp pomfret with litchi 荔枝鲳鱼

Hunan Cuisine 湖南（湘）菜

Steamed turtle 清蒸甲鱼
White bait in chafing dish 银鱼火锅
Braised shark's fin in brown sauce 红煨鱼翅
Sweet lotus seed 冰糖湘莲
Braised dried pork with eel slices 腊肉焖鳝片
Crispy rice crust with sea cucumber 锅巴海参
Spring chicken with cayenne pepper 麻辣子鸡

Anhui Cuisine 安徽菜

Huangshan stewed pigeon 黄山炖鸽
Gourd duck 葫芦鸭子
Fricassee pork sinew with egg white 芙蓉蹄筋

Crispy pork with pine nuts 松子米酥肉
Spicy fried chicken 椒盐米鸡

Zhejiang Food 浙江菜

West Lake vinegar fish 西湖醋鱼
Shelled shrimps with Dragon Well tea leaves 龙井虾仁
West Lake water shied soup 西湖纯菜汤
Eight-jewel rice pudding wrapped with lotus leaves 八宝荷叶饭
Beggar's chicken 叫化鸡
Dongpo Pork 东坡肉

Beijing Food 北京菜

Beijing Roast Duck 北京烤鸭
Rinsed mutton 涮羊肉
Steamed shad 清蒸鲥鱼
Fried shelled shrimps on toast 锅贴虾仁
Almond and milk in jelly 杏仁豆腐

Shanghai Food 上海菜

Braised shark's fins 红烧排翅
Bird's nest shaped as butterfly 蝴蝶燕窝
Chicken with rice flour wrapped in lotus leaf 葱油荷叶粉蒸鸡
Saute shredded chicken and shepherd purse 荠菜鸡丝
Saute shrimp roe and wheat gluten 虾子面筋

References 参考书目

1. 关肇远. 导游英语口语[M]. 北京: 高等教育出版社, 2004.
2. 冯玮, 黄艳. 新编导游英语[M]. 武汉: 武汉大学出版社, 2007.
3. 纪春, 裴松青. 英语导游教程[M]. 北京: 旅游教育出版社, 2007.
4. 段开成. 导游英语听与说[M]. 天津: 南开大学出版社, 2004.
5. 郭兆康. 饭店情景英语[M]. 上海: 复旦大学出版社, 2007.
6. 梅德明. 高级英语口译教程[M]. 上海: 上海外语教育出版社, 2002.
7. 魏国富. 实用旅游英语口语[M]. 上海: 复旦大学出版社, 2004.
8. 朱华. 旅游英语教程[M]. 北京: 高等教育出版社, 2006.
9. 谢先泽. 中国旅游: 英语读本[M]. 成都: 西南财经大学出版社, 2006.
10. 初丽岩. 旅游交际英语通[M]. 上海: 华东师范大学出版社, 2006.
11. 毕洪英. 敢说导游服务英语[M]. 北京: 机械工业出版社, 2006.
12. 苏静. 导游英语[M]. 北京: 化学工业出版社, 2007.
13. 吴云. 旅游实践英语[M]. 北京: 旅游教育出版社, 2007.
14. 杨志忠, 杨义德, 许艾君. 涉外导游英语[M]. 上海: 复旦大学出版社, 2007.
15. 孙小柯. 新编饭店英语[M]. 武汉: 武汉大学出版社, 2007.
16. 姚宝荣. 模拟导游教程[M]. 北京: 中国旅游出版社, 2004.
17. 赵宝国, 谭晓蓉. 21世纪实用旅游英语教程[M]. 上海: 学林出版社, 2005.
18. 吴云, 邵华. 21世纪实用饭店情景英语教程[M]. 上海: 学林出版社, 2005.
19. 南凡. 旅游英语[M]. 北京: 高等教育出版社, 2005.
20. 杨华. 实用旅游英语[M]. 北京: 中国人民大学出版社, 2006.
21. 张靖, 余宝珠. 英语导游基础教程[M]. 北京: 清华大学出版社, 2009.
22. 王浪. 中国著名旅游景区导游词精选[M]. 北京: 旅游教育出版社, 2010.
23. http://www.chinapages.com
24. http://www.ebigear.com
25. http://www.gjgy.com/chinanp.html
26. http://www.fjms.net/masterpiece